Sir John Falstaff

Mistress Page

Well-Loved Tales from Shakespeare

Bernard Miles

Illustrated by
Victor G. Ambrus

Rand McNally & Company
Chicago · New York · San Francisco

To Marsha Bath and her pupils far away in Edmond, Oklahoma, USA who wrote me such delightful letters about my first book of Shakespeare stories – hoping this second crop will give them just as much pleasure.

The illustrations in the Introduction (pages 8 and 10) are based on illustrations in *The Globe Restored* (2nd edition, Oxford University Press, 1968) by C. Walter Hodges, to whom the author, artist and publishers make grateful thanks.

Sycorax

Published in the United States of America
by Rand McNally and Company, 1986

Prepared by
Hamlyn Publishing,
a division of The Hamlyn Publishing Group Limited,
Bridge House, London Road,
Twickenham, Middlesex, England
Copyright © Lord Miles 1986
Copyright © illustrations Hamlyn Publishing 1986
a division of The Hamlyn Publishing Group Limited

Library of Congress Catalog Card Number: 85-63829

ISBN 0-528-82758-8
Printed in Spain

Contents

Introduction   9

The Tempest   12

As You Like It   36

Othello   60

The Merry Wives of Windsor   80

Julius Caesar   104

Mistress Ford

Mistress Page

7

Introduction

The theatre in England started in the arms of the Church in the Middle Ages. The priest read portions of the scriptures aloud, in Latin (of which he sometimes understood as little as his congregation) relying on pictures in the stained glass windows to fill in the actual stories – God creating Adam and Eve, Cain mudering Abel, Noah letting the dove out of the Ark, David killing Goliath, then on to the Annunciation, the Nativity, the Flight into Egypt, the Massacre of the Innocents, and so to the Crucifixion, the Resurrection and the Day of Judgement. Windows in medieval parish churches all over Europe blaze with the Christian story, told in brilliantly coloured glass which is often five or six hundred years old.

Then, perhaps as early as the thirteenth century, someone said, 'Why not re-write the actual scriptures in the form of little plays and perform them in our own language, using the various parts of the church as different places in the story? We could have Adam and Eve in white leather leotards, painted trees for the Garden of Eden, a pretended boat for the Ark and a crib for Baby Jesus, and so on right through to the Day of Judgement, full of demons with pitch forks, tossing wicked souls into the eternal fire for their punishment.' And that is just what they did.

Soon these plays grew so popular that the Church people became jealous and moved them outside the churches. Then the actors built themselves portable platforms and performed in the streets. Later they set up their stages inside inn yards or better still, built enclosures of their own. Then they could charge spectators for admittance and earn a living.

Companies of actors also performed in the houses of great noblemen and each nobleman would take a company under his care, pay its members regular wages and give them a special uniform decorated with his coat of arms, to show who they belonged to. And often their lord would give them some of his cast-off clothing, richer than they could ever afford themselves, and which enabled them to collect a theatre wardrobe.

As the audiences grew bigger the players of Shakespeare's time set about building themselves proper theatres, what we call 'purpose made', a stage planted on trestles with galleries all round

for the audience. On page 8 you see a picture of an open-air street platform with a play in progress, and above, one of a fully grown theatre like the one Shakespeare knew called The Globe, built on the South Bank of the River Thames in London. Theatres had now become so elaborate that someone in the 16th century called them 'gorgeous painted playing places'.

The theatre of Shakespeare's time had no painted scenery, just a few properties, thrones and chairs, pieces of ships, ladders, tree trunks, caves, battlements – just elements of scenery. For the scene was created by the playwright in words. That was his job.

The huge old-fashioned theatres and opera houses we see today, by contrast, are fitted out with as many as 100 sets of strong rope lines, running over pulley wheels high up above the stage, each able to lift ten or twelve hundred-weight of painted scenery up and down during the play – all vastly cumbersome and expensive. This kind of theatre was established in Europe by about 1650 and reigned supreme for more than 200 years, until around 1900 directors and designers began to examine the methods used in Shakespeare's own day and found they gave wider scope for the designer's imagination – besides being more economical in terms of cash.

In the Elizabethan theatre, all the women's parts were played by boys, and you can guess what fun they had dressing up and performing such roles as Rosalind, Celia and Audrey, the two Merry Wives, Miranda and sweet Ann Page!

Shakespeare came from a small English market town, Stratford-upon-Avon, about 100 miles west of London. No one knows how or when he became an actor. All we know is that between about 1590 and 1613 he wrote 37 plays, then retired and went back home to take his ease.

The plays are not easy to read. Remember they were written 400 years ago, when our language and the ways of using it were very different from what they are today. And yet, locked away inside the plays are some of the most exciting stories ever told, some romantic, some tragic, some comic, but all full of interesting people. All I have tried to do is to dig out the stories from which the plays were made and put them back into simple modern language – as a sort of gateway into the magical world of the plays themselves; their violence, their vitality, their freedom, their fun and above all, their glorious language; and I am very lucky to have had my old friend Victor Ambrus to illuminate them with such splendid drawings.

I have here and there added certain details from my own imagination, so the stories don't always follow the plays exactly. But I hope such additions will help make Shakespeare's characters and their world come alive as vividly as if you were watching them being played by live actors, and that they will stay in your imagination for the rest of your lives.

Bernard Miles

Trinculo

Caliban

Stephano

The Tempest

Ariel

Shakespeare came to London around Armada-time, 1588, and retired in 1616. During that quarter century he had written 35 plays, six long narrative poems and 154 sonnets. He enjoyed his retirement in Stratford but still hankered after his much-loved theatres, the Globe and the Blackfriars, and found it hard to sit in his orchard at New Place like Justice Shallow, nodding off after a nice plump capon and a couple of glasses of Canary. Writing had become a habit, almost an addiction. The quills and the pen-knife and the flask of ink and the sheets of clean paper lay temptingly ready on his desk.

Besides, the players were eager for new material. He had served them up such royal dishes over the years and they had played a signal part in setting him free to retire and take his ease. Now his old friends sent persuasive letters and sometimes a personal deputation to Stratford. Just one more? Or perhaps two? Old friends he had worked with over the years in that unique fellowship which is at the heart of all the best theatrical companies – could he really say no?

Shakespeare had lived through momentous events – the final humbling of Spain, Drake's circumnavigation of the globe, the beheading of the Queen's favourite, Essex, Dr Donne's preaching, the building of the Blackfriars theatre and the fearful upheavals in science and religion which we call the Renaissance. He had learned that the world was not a flat disc after all, but a sphere – not the centre of the universe, but a tiny planet circling round a smallish star which was itself one of millions. He had seen the growing influence of the Puritans with their preachers thundering hell-fire sermons at Paul's Cross, claiming that plays and play-acting were the work of the devil, and that all who practised them would go to hell.

Ah, but his plays had been performed at court, and Queen Elizabeth had rocked with laughter at the antics of John Falstaff and his disreputable gang in the two parts of *Henry IV*. He had purchased a gate-house and a parcel of land in Puddle Dock Hill in the City of London. He had become one of the immortal seven who took a lease of the upstairs dining-room of the old monastery hard by and turned it into the first genuine Theatre Royal, not yet so named, but used exclusively by the Queen's men and then by the King's men, between 1595 and 1642.

He had obliged, in 1610, with *The Winter's Tale*. Now they wanted a follow-up. Another play by Master Shakespeare! That would draw the crowds. A comedy? He would see. Perhaps something would occur to him. He would think it over. Then he nodded off.

Out of his dreaming came *The Tempest*. He had written of blood and thunder, of murders and suicides, of death by land and sea, of heroism and betrayal. He had studied mankind in all its variety. He had drunk life to the lees. Hotspur, Lear, Coriolanus, Macbeth and

his murderous lady. What, would the line stretch out to the crack of doom? What kind of play would best express his summing up of life?

So here, in the orchard at Stratford it dawned on him that the greatest gift an old man could possibly wish for would be the end of tumult and strife, an end of Christians burning each other, an end of family feuds, an end of beheadings on Tower Hill, an end of plots to blow up Parliament – a coming together, a clasping of hands, a reconciliation.

As he was accustomed to do, he thumbed through the leather-bound volumes he had picked up over the years in the booksellers around St Paul's, at Henry Carre's over against the Blazing Star, at John Sheppard's at the Brazen Serpent, at Nicholas Ling's and Walter Burre's at the Flower de Luce and Crown, at Christopher Barker's at the Grasshopper, at Thomas Woodcock's – all in St Paul's Churchyard and the streets around. He had copies of Holinshed, Plutarch, books on navigation, Raleigh's *History of the World*, essays on *Drill with Muskets and Swords and Pikes* and all the rest of it. At last he settled upon a story told by an Italian writer named Florio and mixed it with a true account of a voyage to Virginia which had run into a fearful storm, some of its ships being wrecked on an island inhabited by cannibals.

These were the two stories Shakespeare chose, weaving them together to make them his own. This was the play he called *The Tempest*, changed beyond recognition, with the beautiful bird-like Ariel, and Prospero's books of magic and his crystal; starting off with quarrelling and bloodshed and an attempt to drown Prospero and his beloved Miranda, then continuing in his own way without further help. And this is the story he wrote.

It is about a magic shipwreck in a storm that is only a make-believe storm and of things that happen on an enchanted island far out in the ocean many, many years ago.

If you look at a map of Europe, you will see that Italy is shaped like a long boot with the sea on both sides. In the north is the city of Milan, and in the olden days the Duke of Milan ruled a large part of the country, called a province. In those days dukes often went to war with each other and tried to take over each other's provinces.

Now the Duke in this story is called Prospero, and I'm afraid he cannot be bothered to look after his own province, let alone try to take over anyone else's. His wife had died giving birth to a baby girl named Miranda, so in order to forget his sorrow Prospero has taken to studying books of wisdom, full of secret charms and magic spells, leaving the government to his younger brother Antonio.

But Antonio is not content to be just a younger brother. He wants to take Prospero's place and become Duke of Milan himself. All the same he knows the people of Milan love Prospero and would not wish to see him hurt, so Antonio and his friend Alonzo, King of Naples (that was another province, near the south) work out a plan to get rid of Prospero once and for all. And this is how they do it.

Alonzo pretends to attack Milan with a large army, and in the mock fighting Antonio captures Prospero and his baby daughter and gives orders that they shall be cast adrift in a tiny boat without sails or oars, miles out at sea, to starve or perhaps to drown. Then he tells the people of Milan that Prospero and Miranda have been killed in the fighting, and soon afterwards he has himself made Duke.

One of his courtiers named Gonzalo is ordered to carry out this cruel plot. But he loves Prospero, and although he does not disobey Antonio's orders, he secretly puts food and clothing on board the little boat before it is cast adrift, together with Prospero's books of wisdom and magic charms, and most important of all, his globe of pure crystal which, if you look carefully into it, will show you what is happening all over the world. You have only to hold it in a certain way and by concentrating set up vibrations which correspond to your thoughts – in other words you have to 'tune in'. After years of practice, Prospero has become adept at this mysterious art.

Prospero and his baby daughter, blown this way and that by the rough seas, at last drift down onto a tiny island far out in the ocean, and there they live for twelve long years; Prospero reading and studying his books of magic, Miranda growing up to be a beautiful young woman, learning about the sea birds, the cormorants, the shags, the gannets, and the humming birds which thumb a lift under the wings of albatross and travel thousands of miles from

Prospero

Miranda

17

Sycorax

Spain or Africa. Also the trees, and the varied flowers and grasses – and the glorious butterflies, many of them as big as swallows. Prospero gives her an hour's schooling each day, teaching her how to read and write, and how to draw patterns with his compasses, and how to cut up pieces of parchment into rectangles and triangles and pentacles.

Now I must tell you something about this island. You will never find it on a map because it is an enchanted island that once belonged to an old witch named Sycorax, one of the wickedest witches that ever lived. In fact she was so old and so wicked that she gradually got bent into a circle. If you were brave enough and strong enough you could bowl her along the road like a hoop. And if you could fasten her on an axle with her wicked sister Hecate who lived up in the north of Scotland you could use them for wheels on a carriage, and that would serve them right.

Now it so happens that Sycorax had a son called Caliban, and he's the ugliest creature you could ever see, covered with rough hair and scales, savage and slow-witted. No-one knows who his father is. All they know is that one night at full moon a terrible howling was heard coming from the middle of a dark wood. In the morning Sycorax came out dragging Caliban after her by the scruff of his neck, claiming that he was her son. He's not as wicked as his mother, but is a sort of monster, with webbed hands and feet, half-way between a man and an ape, with a bit of fish mixed in.

When Sycorax first came to the island it was a happy place with only good fairies living there. But she soon put a stop to that. She bullied the fairies and ordered them about, and when they refused to do everything she told them, she punished them by trapping them inside hollow trees or under heavy stones, leaving them without anything to eat or drink, sometimes for years on end.

The chief of these good fairies is Ariel, and when he refused to do some of the nasty things Sycorax ordered, she split a great pine tree wide open and fastened him inside it with only his head showing, so that he couldn't get out. Poor Ariel is so fine and delicate you can hardly see him. He has pale blue eyes and delicate golden hair, and he is so nimble he can move like a flash of light – very different from ugly bound-up-like-a-hoop old Sycorax. There he is, fixed inside this pine tree, unable to move, with Caliban free to mock him and poke at him with a stick and make jokes about him, not spitefully, but mostly out of curiosity, to see how loud he can make Ariel scream.

Then one day Sycorax died, for even witches don't go on living for ever. So poor, half-witted Caliban is in charge of the island. But not for long, because Prospero and Miranda come drifting in from the open sea in their little boat and soon set up home there.

Now Prospero knows as much about magic as Sycorax had ever known. The difference is that his is a good magic, hers a bad one; in fact hers was thoroughly wicked. Prospero hears Ariel and the other fairies screaming with pain so he hacks open the trees and lifts the great stones and sets them all free. And the fairies are so happy they promise to be his faithful servants for as long as he stays on the island. Ariel is so delighted to escape from his torment that he promises Prospero to be the best servant of all, a sort of personal assistant. Prospero is glad to accept his help and promises that one day he will set him free for ever. He can't do it yet, because he has a plan of his own for getting off the island and back to his kingdom and he will need Ariel's help to make it work.

Prospero and Miranda make their home in a big, dry cave overlooking the long, sandy beach and the blue-green sea. It has ferns and flowers all round it, and sweet-smelling creepers tumbling down across its front like a curtain. Inside, there are three smaller caves, each one leading off the big one. Prospero turns the main cave into a sort of living-room, one of the little ones into a bedroom and workroom for himself and another one into a kitchen. But the nicest little cave of all he turns into Miranda's room. It is very tiny but it has a stone shelf that sticks out like a wide mantelpiece, where she can sleep. Fancy going to sleep on a mantelpiece!

Then he takes his boat to pieces and uses the timbers to make some furniture; a table and two stools, a desk where he can work and a little ladder for Miranda so that she can climb up to her bed. She is still very small, remember, not yet four years old, and the stone shelf is quite a long way off the ground. So he fixes a little handrail all the way to the top, so she can hold onto it as she climbs the ladder to go to sleep. And he fastens a fillet to the edge of the shelf so she can't roll off in the night. It's really a sort of stone bunk, very cosy and comfortable.

Miranda

Miranda

Caliban

20

Caliban is angry when Prospero comes to the island. Just when he thinks he's got it all to himself here is this magician and his baby daughter butting in and spoiling everything. After all it's his island, not theirs. All the same, he does his best to be friendly. He shows Prospero where to find nice clear water and where the best fruits and nuts and berries grow. So Prospero makes him into a sort of handyman, to fetch firewood and fresh water, and keep the cave clean and tidy.

Prospero tries to teach Caliban manners, but I'm afraid he isn't very successful. Caliban simply will not stop eating with his fingers and slopping his soup all over the table. Miranda too, as she grows older, does her best to help Caliban, showing him how to write his name in big capital letters, and how to build sand castles and play what he calls 'heed and sike' (he never does learn to say 'hide and seek'). She even tries to teach him to drink out of a cup instead of lapping it up like a puppy dog.

But somehow poor old Caliban can't manage it. He will knock down the sand castles and splosh water all over them, and when she isn't looking he will pinch Miranda's legs and pull her hair, just like a naughty little boy. He doesn't do it on purpose. It seems he just can't help it. It's his nature, like tormenting poor Ariel when he was fastened inside the pine tree. He won't even let Miranda cut his fingernails which are like claws. And when she stands over him and gives him a really good wash, he will go straight out of the cave and roll on the ground and make himself dirty all over again. Even when Miranda tries to make him speak properly, all he does is grunt and say rude words.

So as Miranda grows older and more beautiful, Prospero stops Caliban from coming into his home altogether and makes him live by himself in another little cave, with Ariel to watch over him and make him behave himself. When he's slow in gathering firewood or carrying water, Ariel pinches him or shouts in his ear, 'Keep

moving! I'm watching you!' But most of the time Ariel and the
other fairies sing to each other and play their magic flutes as they
dance up and down in the treetops or flit like birds around
Caliban's head. Caliban likes music so that makes him very happy.
Sometimes he even tries to join in, but he can only manage a sort of
howling, rather like a dog that doesn't like being chained up.

Now as I told you, Prospero is a very clever magician. He has a
magic crystal, made of a special substance called quartz, as smooth
as glass and as cold as ice; and looking in his crystal one day he
suddenly sees a ship sailing towards the island. On the ship are his
wicked brother Antonio, who has stolen his kingdom, and

Alonzo, King of Naples, who helped him; also Alonzo's son, Ferdinand, now grown into a fine young man. With them are Alonzo's brother Sebastian, and Lord Gonzalo, the old courtier who had been so kind when Prospero and Miranda were cast adrift.

'Ha!' cries Prospero. 'Now I've got them!' And he waves his magic wand, raising a mighty storm which whips the seas up into huge waves, driving the ship straight towards the rocky coast. (This is the tempest from which the play gets its name. Shakespeare puts this bit of the story at the beginning of the play in order to start it off with a bang and catch the audience's attention, but it should happen now and I think it better to put it here.)

When Miranda looks into her father's crystal and sees the ship fighting the storm, its masts bending in the gale and its sails being torn to ribbons, she cries, 'Oh, Father, look! That beautiful ship will be smashed on the rocks and all the people aboard her will be lost! Can't you save her?'

Prospero smiles and takes her hand. 'Don't worry, my darling,' he says. 'I have sent Ariel to watch over her. Although the ship seems lost he will save her, and he will see that no one on board comes to any harm.' Then he draws her to his side and tells her who he really is and who she is and how they came to be on the island, adding that on the ship are the very people who drove him out of his kingdom. He does not want to hurt them, only to teach them a lesson. Miranda need not worry, she can leave everything to Ariel. Then Prospero waves his wand over her and she falls asleep.

On board the ship Ariel is busy flitting up and down the masts in flashes of lightning like St Elmo's Fire, and making the thunder that follows it sound like the ship's timbers being wrenched apart, so that everyone on board is sure she has struck the rocks and is breaking up. It is only a make-believe storm, but they are all terribly frightened. It is early morning. Most of them are still in their night clothes and every time they try to get back to their cabins, the ship gives a great lurch and nearly throws them overboard. Then the next wave washes right over the ship, half drowning them.

A huge wave catches Prince Ferdinand and carries him over the side and he soon disappears in the breakers. Then the water washes right over the decks, sweeping everybody into the angry seas. There they are, bobbing about like corks in a bathtub; only their long cloaks and dressing gowns keeping them afloat; eyes and mouths full of salt water, trying to cling to the barrels and spars and odds and ends of furniture that swept overboard with them.

Stephano, Alonzo's butler, a fat little man with a very red nose, manages to climb onto a half-empty wine barrel, and is riding the waves in fine style when a huge breaker catches him and tosses him high up on to the beach. You will hear more about Stephano and his wine barrel later.

Prospero watches all this in his crystal and chuckles to himself. 'That will teach them a lesson!' he says. But he makes sure they all come to land unharmed except for the soaking they had, and the ship remains intact. Then he tells Ariel to guide them all, passengers and crew, to different parts of the island, so that they will all think they are the only ones saved.

Antonio, Alonzo and his brother Sebastian are washed ashore together, and a few moments later poor old Gonzalo staggers up the beach after them, soaked to the skin. Fearing that Ferdinand, who was the first to be washed overboard, must surely have drowned, Alonzo and Gonzalo wander wearily up and down the beach looking for his body. At last they give up, feeling sure he is lost for ever, and sit down among the rocks to rest and dry themselves in the sun. They are no longer young and they had a rough time in the water; the sun has just risen and they are so glad to be still alive that they soon grow weary and drop off to sleep.

But Antonio and Sebastian stay awake, and as they walk along the beach, wicked thoughts come into their heads. Antonio whispers that now is Sebastian's chance to get rid of his brother Alonzo and so become King of Naples himself. No one will ever know. If only they can escape from the island and get back home again, they can tell everyone that Alonzo and Ferdinand had both drowned in the shipwreck. Of course, they will have to kill old Gonzalo too. There mustn't be any witnesses to their crime. But he is only an old courtier. No-one will bother about him. He won't even be missed!

All the time Prospero is watching them in his crystal, and Ariel is hovering in the air above them, listening to their plot. So just as they draw their swords and are about to plunge them into Alonzo and poor old Gonzalo, Ariel pinches the two sleepers and wakes them up.

'Why, whatever are you two doing with your swords drawn?' asks Alonzo, coming to with a start.

'Oh, we heard a lion roaring close by,' says Antonio. 'You must have heard it in your sleep, and that's what woke you.'

Of course it's a lie, but Alonzo and Gonzalo believe it. 'It's lucky you two were awake to protect us,' says Alonzo. 'And it's a good thing I was awake watching over them,' chuckles Ariel to himself as he flies back to tell Prospero everything that has happened.

'Yes, I saw it all in my crystal,' says Prospero. 'You are a clever little spirit. Now let's see what the others are up to.' And he switches his magic glass to another part of the island. Then he begins to chuckle, for he can see Trinculo, Alonzo's jester. In the old days kings and lords all employed clever men called jesters, to keep them amused, to tell them funny stories and do conjuring tricks, like the clowns in a circus.

This Trinculo is as thin as a beanpole, with big ears and a very long nose. You would laugh to see him, especially now when he's

24

wet through from his dip in the sea and feeling very sorry for himself. He's looking for his friend Stephano, Alonzo's butler, whom he had last seen riding the surf on top of a barrel. Stephano is bound to have some wine with him and Trinculo could do with a nice long drink to warm him up.

As he wanders along, wet and cold and tired out, he suddenly sees Caliban sheltering under his rough goatskin cloak. He has pulled it over his head but left his big hairy feet sticking out at the end. 'What sort of head would fit onto a pair of feet like those?' wonders Trinculo, and he is just about to lift up the other end of the cloak and have a look when he hears a roll of thunder and it starts to pour with rain again.

'Oh,' cries Trinculo, 'another wetting!' and he looks around for some shelter. But there are no trees in sight and all the bushes are still dripping from the last downpour. 'I think I'll get under this strange creature's cloak,' he says to himself. 'You can't pick and choose your bedfellows at a time like this.' And he crawls under the cloak at the opposite end from Caliban's feet and begins to make himself comfortable. So here is this old goatskin cloak with Caliban's feet sticking out at one end and Trinculo's at the other. It really is a most peculiar sight.

Stephano the butler certainly thinks so, as he comes staggering along carrying a leather flask which he has filled with some of the wine from his barrel. He's been taking sips all the way up the beach and is now very tipsy. So when he sees the two pairs of legs sticking out from under the cloak he thinks he must be seeing double.

'Whatever's this?' he asks himself, stirring the strange object

Trinculo

with his foot and spilling some of the precious wine over Trinculo's feet. 'A hairy monster with four legs, two as thin as matchsticks and two as thick as tree-trunks! I wonder where his head can be?'

At that, Trinculo puts his head out from one side of the goatskin and Caliban his from the other. Four legs and now two heads – whatever next?

'Why, if it isn't my dear old pal Trinculo!' splutters Stephano. 'How happy I am to find you still alive! Who's your ugly friend?'

'Oh, he's a monster I happened to come across,' says Trinculo. 'He smells awful, but I think he's quite harmless.' Then he crawls out from under the cloak and joins hands with Stephano and the two of them dance a little jig round the astonished Caliban, only just managing to keep each other on an even keel.

'Have a drink, monster,' says the tipsy butler, offering the flask, and Caliban takes a good swig. He has never tasted anything stronger than water before and the wine is sweet and very strong. 'Surely,' he thinks, 'surely this man with the wonderful drink must be a god!' Then, with a gulp and a giggle, Stephano offers Caliban another swig. So he drinks again, and of course the wine goes straight to his head and he gets very tipsy. He loves this funny fat little man. But he doesn't think much of the tall man with the long nose who keeps poking fun at him. Stephano doesn't make fun of him. Stephano gives him drinks from that wonderful flask.

But the drink puts awful thoughts into his head, and I'll tell you what they are. If only they can get rid of Prospero, they will make Stephano King of the Island and serve him instead. After all, the island really belongs to Caliban. Prospero has stolen it from him.

Caliban

27

Miranda

Ferdinand

28

Why shouldn't they catch Prospero while he's asleep and batter his brains in with a log of wood or a great stone? He blurts all this out in his mumbling, stumbling drunken voice between gulps at the wine, waiting for Stephano to drink, then as soon as Trinculo tries to get a mouthful, snatching the flask away from him.

Stephano listens to the strange monster. He feels flattered and pleased. It's nice to be made to feel important, even by such an ugly creature as Caliban, so he agrees to everything Caliban says. They will kill the monster's master and then Stephano will become King of the Island and Caliban will be his Prime Minister. But first of all they must refill the flask. Killing powerful magicians like Prospero is thirsty work.

So back they go to the wine barrel, not knowing that Ariel has heard their silly drunken plot and flown straight back to tell Prospero all about it. Prospero laughs and tells Ariel to bewitch the three rogues so that they can't find their way to his cave but will wander around until they land up in a swamp where they will stick fast in the mud.

Now while all this is happening, Ferdinand has come ashore close to Prospero's cave. As he wades up the beach and sees great waves bursting over the ship, he feels sure that his father and the whole ship's company must have drowned and this makes him very sad.

He's walking along, soaked to the skin and feeling very sorry for himself, when he hears strange music in the air, but can't make out where it's coming from. Sometimes it seems to come from one side, sometimes from the other, sometimes from the sky and sometimes from underground. He doesn't know of course that the music is leading him straight to Prospero's cave.

When Miranda sees Ferdinand coming towards her, she's astonished. The only grown-up creatures she has ever seen are her father and Caliban, so she cries out in wonder at the sight of this young man, so young and handsome but looking so very sad. And when Ferdinand sees Miranda he's astonished too, seeing such a beautiful girl in that wild and lonely place. He thinks he has never before set eyes on anyone so lovely.

It is clear to Prospero, as he stands by watching them, that they have already fallen deeply in love with each other. But to find out if this young man is worthy of his precious daughter, he decides to put him to the test. He speaks roughly to Ferdinand and won't listen to a word of his story. Then he tells him that if he wants any food, he must work for it.

So, before he knows what he's doing, poor Ferdinand finds himself doing Caliban's job, carrying logs into the cave, then chopping them up for the fire. He does this without a murmur, his eyes fixed lovingly on Miranda. In fact, he is so busy looking at her, instead of getting on with his work that he nearly chops one of his fingers off and Miranda has to bind it up with her handkerchief,

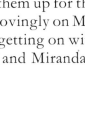

whispering as she does so that her father is not really as bad-tempered as he seems. Then she begins to help Ferdinand carry the logs. When he sees this, Prospero smiles even more, delighted that everything is going just as he has planned.

Now while all this is happening, Ariel has been playing a wicked trick on Alonzo and Sebastian and Antonio. There they are, tired, hungry and thirsty, wandering round looking for Ferdinand's body and beginning to fear that they will starve to death, when suddenly a marvellous banquet is spread out before them; wines and fruits and ice-cream and pastry and jellies, all set out on a fine table with knives and forks of pure gold. But then, just as they are about to sit down and enjoy this delicious meal, Ariel comes flying down across the table, flaps his wings over it and makes it all disappear. One moment it's there and their mouths are watering at the thought of sitting down to eat and drink, then it has vanished and Ariel is standing tiptoe on a fallen tree-trunk giving them a stern lecture.

He reminds them of the wrongs they have done to Prospero. It seems he knows every detail of their wickedness. What a fix they're in now! Alonzo's son lost, and the rest of them cast up on an enchanted island with no hope of ever getting back home, and this strange birdlike spirit knows all about their wicked past. And now that the feast has disappeared, they are feeling hungrier and thirstier than ever.

Caliban

Stephano

Trinculo

30

Old Gonzalo has seen nothing of the feast nor of Ariel. He has dropped off to sleep again. So when he wakes up he asks Alonzo why he looks so unhappy. 'Oh, Gonzalo,' says Alonzo, 'I realise how badly I have behaved towards the noble Prospero and his little daughter! And now as a punishment I am lost on this desert island and my dear son is drowned and I shall never see Naples again.'

Antonio also hangs his head in shame, for he remembers how he and Sebastian tried to kill Alonzo and Gonzalo when they were asleep.

But what about poor Caliban and his two friends? How are they getting on? Well, Prospero decided to teach them a lesson too, like this. He tells Ariel to collect all the bright-coloured clothes and scarves and pretty trinkets from the cave and hang them on the bushes that shelter it. Then he tells Ariel to go and help Caliban, Trinculo and Stephano out of the swamp, while he pretends to go to sleep.

Soon the trio come into sight, plastered with dirt and still very tipsy. And of course, when they see the fine garments hanging outside the cave, they want to try them on. Caliban does his best to stop them, telling them they must first get rid of Prospero, but they take no notice.

Stephano wraps himself in a fine embroidered cloak, then trips up and falls over and rolls on the ground. Trinculo tries on a jewelled crown, but it's far too big for him and it falls over his ears. Caliban begs them to stop dressing themselves up until they have killed Prospero. 'He'll be waking up any minute now, we must do it while he's still asleep!' he says. But they take no notice, dancing about in their fine clothes as if they are already lords of the island.

Of course Prospero isn't really asleep. He's watching them all the time. And he can't help laughing, especially when Trinculo and Stephano begin to quarrel over who should wear what, and Caliban begins to scold them, asking how they can be such fools as to waste time trying on pretty clothes when any moment Prospero might wake up and catch them.

So to bring them to their senses, Ariel whistles up a pack of magic hounds which snap at their heels and chase them off into the woods, yelling with fright. It really is so funny I'm sure you'll laugh as much as Ariel does.

But now Prospero has to put an end to this strange tale of magic and enchantment. He dresses up in his magician's robes and sends Ariel to bring Antonio and Alonzo and the others towards the cave. Since they now seem so sorry for all the harm they have done he has decided to forgive them.

When they first see Prospero, they can hardly believe their eyes. They think they must be dreaming. But Prospero soon proves that he's no dream, and Alonzo and Antonio go down on their knees and beg forgiveness for all the wrongs they have done.

Alonzo tells Prospero how he has lost his dear son Ferdinand and Prospero says he knows how sad Alonzo must be feeling because he himself has lost his precious Miranda.

'Then your loss, on top of all you have suffered, is far greater than mine,' says Alonzo. 'Oh, how I wish my son and your daughter were still alive. I would give up my Kingdom and make them King and Queen of it!'

Of course Prospero doesn't really mean that his daughter is dead, only that he has lost her to Ferdinand. For suddenly he pulls aside a curtain at the back of the cave where the two young lovers are sitting hand in hand, telling each other of their adventures since they left Italy and drifted down to the island, ending with the admission that they have fallen deeply in love one with the other and pray that they may soon become man and wife.

When they see Alonzo and Antonio and Sebastian, Ferdinand and Miranda are amazed. Miranda has never seen so many human beings before, and Ferdinand, who is sure his father and all the others have been lost in the shipwreck, is so happy he can hardly speak. He takes Miranda by the hand and presents her to his father as his chosen bride, the Duke of Milan's daughter and the future Queen of Naples. And Alonzo joins their hands and promises them a truly wonderful wedding if ever they get back home.

But then, would you believe it, whom should Ariel lead into the cave but the Captain and the Mate of the ship. She's not really been wrecked at all, but has been riding safely at anchor in a little harbour close by, along with her crew. The storm and the shipwreck have all been part of Prospero's magic. Their whole beings, eyes and ears and feelings have been caught up and imprisoned in a world made of Prospero's thoughts and dreams of long-remembered injustices, crystallised into this strange pattern of experiences.

Now there is only one thing more to be done. Caliban, Trinculo and Stephano are still running away from the cave, frightened out of their wits that the hounds will attack them again. So Prospero sends Ariel off to fetch them, and very soon they appear. And what a sight they look, their fine clothes all torn and their hands and faces so dirty you can hardly recognise them. But Prospero is too happy to be angry with them. He simply orders them to put back all the things they have taken, tidy up the cave, then go and get the supper ready.

While they are eating, Prospero tells them how in his crystal, he saw their ship arriving and how by his magic he raised the storm in order to bring them all under his control and punish them for all their past wickedness. Everyone listens spellbound to his tale of mystery and enchantment. And when supper is over he makes Caliban, Stephano and Trinculo clear away and do the washing up!

When everyone is asleep Prospero sits at his table, trying to decide how much longer to pursue his magic art. He has his Dukedom back, he has made friends of his enemies, his beloved daughter will soon be Queen of Naples and his old friend Gonzalo will once more become his faithful helper. After much pondering, he resolves to give up his magic powers and rejoin the world of ordinary men, helping them to battle with the daily problems of living.

In the morning soon after dawn, just before they leave the island, he dons his ceremonial robe for the last time and calls everyone out on to the beach. Hurling his book of spells and his magic crystal far out to sea he raises his staff aloft and in a ringing voice renounces forever his life as an enchanter, vowing to rejoin the world of common men.

'I'll break my staff,' he cries,
Bury it certain fathoms in the earth,
And deeper than did ever plummet sound,
I'll drown my book.'

Prospero

A sudden flash of lightning strikes his staff, splintering it into a thousand fragments. Then comes a long roll of thunder, as if setting nature's seal upon his vow.

'But what about Caliban?' you ask. Well, Prospero leaves behind a couple of exercise books and some pencils and a pair of proper trousers on the island. And Ariel promises to teach him to read and do joined-up writing and simple sums. But in the end he has to give it up. Poor Caliban can't even learn his ABC. He gets stuck at 'K'. 'K for Kaliban,' he says, 'that's enough for me.'

Nor is he any good at counting. He can manage up to ten on his fingers, but after that he's hopeless. He says 'Seven, eight, nine, ten, twenty-three, thirty-seven, fifty-two-and-a-half and that makes twelve!' It's all very well, he thinks, for Ariel and Prospero and other clever people to read and do arithmetic, but what need has he for such nonsense? He has plenty to eat and lovely spring water to drink (no more of that horrible strong wine Stephano gave him – that made his head ache) and he can sleep in the sun and bathe in the sea. What more can anyone want?

So Ariel gives up trying to teach him and flies thirty-five times round the earth to stretch his wings, leaving our friend Caliban drowsily chewing a blade of grass, with his back to a tree, his legs spread out before him, happily doing his best not to think about anything at all. He's got his island back at last.

As for Ariel, he's still flying across the trees and over the wide sky, mostly invisible. But sometimes he may come in at your bedroom window when you are asleep and perch on the cupboard or the bookshelf and sing one of his beautiful songs, asking you to come and play with him and his fellow spirits on the long strip of yellow sand that runs down to the sea. But if you wake up and look for him he'll slip on his magic coat and disappear, leaving only a few notes of music still hanging in the air. Listen carefully and you may hear them. If you do you will have good luck for a whole year!

Rosalind

Celia

As You Like It

Touchstone

Shakespeare

I have an idea that Shakespeare wrote this play for a wager. Talking together in the Mermaid Tavern after a performance of his *Two Gentlemen of Verona*, a bystander said, 'I'll bet you couldn't write a play about four pairs of lovers, Will!' – they all knew him by his Christian name – 'Or even three,' said the barman.

'How much would you bet?' replied Shakespeare.

'Ten yards of Damask,' said a fellow who happened to be a liveryman of the Mercers' Company, 'fresh from the Indies.'

'Done!' answered Shakespeare. Ten yards of Damask would make a fine present to take home to Stratford-on-Avon for his wife and daughter. Such rarities weren't often seen in country towns a hundred miles from London.

'And one of the girls in the play dresses up as a boy!' said another man standing by, and everyone laughed, because they knew that in the Elizabethan theatre *all* the girls had to be dressed-up boys. Anyway, the wager was agreed and they all shook hands on it.

Most of Shakespeare's plays had been based on stories by foreign writers, Italians or Spaniards, or English historians like Hall or Holinshed, or the Greek chronicler Plutarch. Until now his only English story had been *The Merry Wives of Windsor* so he had to put on his thinking-cap and dream up something really special. And *As You Like It*, one of the most enchanting of all comedies, is the result.

The play is set in the Never Never Land that mankind has dreamed of for hundreds of years – a land where we can get away from it all, living the simple life amongst woodlands and cornfields and meadows full of flowers, in which lovers walk hand in hand and whisper their love to each other and feel each other's heartbeats matching their own.

The Never Never Land of the play, called the Forest of Arden, is really the glorious countryside of Shakespeare's boyhood, except that he never tells us in what county or even in what country it is to be found. All we know is that the old and kindly duke who formerly ruled it has quarrelled with his young brother Frederick, that Frederick has driven him from his throne, that he has gone to live in this beautiful forest like Robin Hood and his Merry Men, and that many of his courtiers flock to join him every day.

Although the duke and his brother have quarrelled and the younger one, Frederick, has driven his brother from the kingdom, they each have a daughter and these two daughters, Rosalind, daughter of the old duke, and Celia, Frederick's daughter, love one another so dearly and delight so much in each other's company, that they refuse to be separated, and Rosalind continues to live in the palace knowing full well that if Duke Frederick – as he now calls himself – were to turn her out, his daughter Celia would follow her.

Not far away there live two other brothers, Oliver and Orlando, sons of Sir Rowland dc Boys who has only recently died. And this Oliver has managed to trick his brother Orlando out of his rightful share of their father's estate, leaving him hungry and ill-clad and poorly educated, so that he scarcely knows where to turn to keep body and soul together. Then, by chance, his ill luck changes.

A professional wrestler is going round the country challenging anyone brave enough to take him on; and to provide some amusement for himself and his courtiers, Duke Frederick has engaged him to wrestle on the palace lawn.

Now, although Orlando often goes hungry, he is lithe and strong and, from the physical work which his brother forces him to do, in hard condition; so when he hears of this wrestler coming to challenge the local youth, he decides to try his luck. The wrestler, whose name is Charles, seeing how young Orlando is, tries to dissuade him and even begs Orlando's brother Oliver to do likewise, but Oliver declines to interfere. Indeed he says he will be only too happy if Charles breaks Orlando's neck.

On the lawn the ring has been marked out. Duke Frederick is seated in a handsome oaken chair with a tray of wine and sweetmeats at his side, while Charles, stripped to the waist, is being pummelled by his two handlers. He is a man of mighty girth, but badly out of condition and quite flabby. A few yards away Orlando has also removed his shirt and stands waiting for the signal to begin. When dressed we thought him a little too slight but now

Rosalind

that we can see his arms and shoulders tapering down to his waist, he looks a very formidable customer indeed – maybe not as heavy as one would wish, but in fine condition and carrying not a single ounce of extra weight.

When Rosalind and Celia see Charles and Orlando stripped and ready for action, they also fear for Orlando's safety and try to dissuade him from fighting. But he has made up his mind to try his luck and at last the match begins.

Orlando

Charles

For a few moments the contestants circle one another, then Charles rushes at Orlando like a mad bull, but Orlando ducks at the last moment and Charles lands on Orlando's back. With all his strength Orlando suddenly straightens himself out like a steel spring, hurling Charles high into the air so that he comes crashing down on his back. As he rises, Orlando catches him with two fast arm-rolls, a head-mare and a monkey climb; then leaps high into the air and lands a twin-footed drop kick to the head and Charles crashes to the ground and fails to get up. The Duke, fearful that Charles may be killed if the fight continues, cries 'Enough, enough!' and Charles is carried out of the ring by his handlers unconscious while Orlando slips on his shirt and prepares to leave.

But Rosalind and Celia call him back to congratulate him, and Rosalind even takes a golden chain from her own neck and hangs it over his with the words: 'Sir, you have wrestled well, and overthrown more than your enemies.'

Orlando looks into her eyes where the meaning of her words is plain to see. She has fallen in love with him – and he with her. Indeed Celia has great difficulty in pulling Rosalind away, leaving Orlando breathless and speechless at this turn of events.

Suddenly, one of Duke Frederick's courtiers breaks the spell. His name is Le Beau and he comes to warn Orlando that Duke Frederick is furious that his champion has been so easily overthrown and intends to do Orlando some mischief if he possibly can. Orlando had better make himself scarce.

Orlando thanks him but doesn't seem to take much notice. He wants to know which of the two beautiful girls he has just met is daughter to Duke Frederick and who is the other one? Le Beau tells him that the smaller of the two, the dark one, belongs to Duke Frederick; the other, Rosalind, who has given him the gold chain, is the daughter of Frederick's banished brother, now living in the Forest of Arden; and that Frederick only tolerates Rosalind at court because she and his Celia are inseparable and it would break Celia's heart if Rosalind were sent away to join her father. He adds that in any case Celia is so popular around the court and amongst the local people, and Frederick so evil and unpredictable, that he might at any moment take it into his head to banish her as well.

Scarcely has Le Beau finished speaking than Duke Frederick himself appears, his brow furrowed with anger, to tell Rosalind that she is no longer welcome at court. He gives her ten days to pack her belongings and say her farewells. If by that time she is not gone, she will be put to death. Her father was a traitor and it is more than likely she is a traitor, too. It is useless to argue. That is his decree. Celia tries to plead with him but the Duke will not be swayed. Rosalind must go.

When the Duke has departed, Celia announces that if Rosalind is banished then she herself is banished too, and when Rosalind asks where they can possibly go, Celia offers a simple and logical solution: 'To seek your father in the forest of Arden!'

They will dress themselves in poor and mean attire, and dirty their faces with amber so that they look as hum-drum as possible. Then Rosalind picks up the idea and embroiders it. 'I know' she says excitedly. 'I, being the taller, will dress as a man, arm myself with a boar spear and an axe, and we'll pretend to be husband and wife. If I can manage to look fierce enough we'll be safe against robbers or footpads or gypsies.'

Finally, Celia caps it all by suggesting that they should persuade Duke Frederick's jester, Touchstone, to join them saying, 'He'll go along o'er the wide world with me.'

So off they go to get their belongings together, break the news to Touchstone and prepare for life in the greenwood.

It is a lucky job Celia thinks of taking Touchstone along for he has some of the best ideas for helping them with their plan. First of all he insists that Rosalind and Celia should prepare their disguises

Rosalind

42

Touchstone

properly and thoroughly rehearse them. Only then will he take the responsibility for this mad adventure.

He himself will remain a clown, but a humbler one such as you might meet in a village or small market town, a kind of inspired village idiot, or a promising local lad hoping one day to make the big time. A sort of apprentice.

The first thing they must do is change Rosalind's shape. She has a lovely top half and a fine swaggering pair of hips, but her small waist (only 18½ inches!) would betray her, and however she walks or sits or stands, you would always know she was not a man.

It is Touchstone who thinks of it. 'Padding,' he says. They must give her an addition, specially shaped and carefully moulded, to fit round her middle and fasten at the front. Then she will need long hose, a stout leather jerkin and a pair of strong walking shoes. And finally they must find her a curtle axe and a boar spear.

'What about luggage?' asks Celia. 'A change of clothes, a pair of blankets, a scrubbing brush, scissors, dinner knives, needles and thread. . .'

'And warm cloaks,' says Rosalind, 'The forest is chilly in winter.'

So they set to work collecting everything they might need for living out in the wild and stow it away in secret ready for packing. Then comes the question: 'What to pack it in?' Rosalind has an old canvas satchel and Celia a large shoulder bag as big as a sack. Then Touchstone produces a battered tin trunk from the palace rubbish dump, and a couple of yards of strong fish-net which they make into another sack, to hold the blankets. Lastly three warm cloaks ready for the winter and one of Rosalind's old felt hats with the brim cut off, making a tight little Robin Hood cap to tuck her golden curls in. Even so, Rosalind would never pass for a man. What else could they do? And it is Touchstone who says they must make her a beard and moustache – and making these proves not as difficult as you might imagine.

First they cut off three or four inches of Rosalind's hair and lay it carefully on the table. Then Celia cuts a piece off her white lace petticoat and makes it into a moustache shape, then makes another piece into a cone shape, just the right size for Rosalind's chin. Then Touchstone takes a piece of glue from the palace carpenter's tool box and thins it down into gum with hot water. Finally they take little tufts of the hair and gum them into place on the two lace shapes and trim them both to look nice and manly.

When all is done and the beard and moustache pressed home with a towel, even Rosalind's best friends would not recognise her, especially when she puts on a deep manly voice.

They spend two whole days rehearsing, Touchstone looking for all the little mistakes that might give them away. But at last he pronounces that they will pass muster and when the moon is up they can safely be on their way.

Only one thing is missing. 'Shouldn't we pack our party dresses and some nice shoes and a few of our favourite jewels?' says Rosalind.

'Whatever for?' asks Celia.

'Just in case . . .' replies Rosalind.

'In case of what?' says Touchstone.

'Well you never know,' says Rosalind rather lamely.

Touchstone and Celia both think it is rather stupid, but they slip back upstairs and re-pack, folding Celia's pink dress and Rosalind's powder blue one carefully in the trunk, followed by Celia's jewel box and their light evening slippers. At last all is ready and the three runaways creep out of the front door, darting silently from shadow to shadow until they are clear of the palace gates.

Only Betty, Duke Frederick's toothless old mastiff (named after Queen Elizabeth) gives a few short howls (not over loud) as they pass her kennel, then they are on their way, long before dawn, out of danger.

Without more ado we plunge straight into the Forest. And what a forest it is. Untouched by man except for the clearing in front of the old Duke's cavern and the wide expanse of meadowland where Corin's sheep may safely graze. Oak, beech, holly, hickory, ash and apple, elbowing each other aside for extra earth and air, rich with violets and primroses, bluebells and campion, orchids and ragged robin, the sky alive with all manner of birds and the whole forest quite overcanopied with wild woodbine, with sweet muskroses and with eglantine. Here the banished duke is telling a group of his courtiers how lucky they all are to have given up the 'painted pomp' of fashion and be living the free and easy outdoor life which finds, 'Tongues in trees, books in the running brooks, sermons in stones, and good in everything.'

His courtiers agree and one of them describes how only an hour or two ago he saw a stag that had received a nasty wound from a local huntsman, come to drink at one of the Forest streams and how the herd to which this poor beast belonged came trotting past him as if he didn't exist.

'Yes,' says the Duke. 'That's just how the world works. Fair enough when you're in the swim, but when you're down on your luck, nobody wants to know you.'

Back at the palace Duke Frederick, learning that Rosalind and Celia have disappeared along with Touchstone, and that the young wrestler who nearly beat the life out of Charles is also missing, gives orders to Orlando's brother Oliver to hunt them down and bring them back.

Conn

Silvius

After the wrestling match, Orlando made his way back to the tumbledown cottage where his brother Oliver forces him to live, and there, waiting for him, is Adam, the faithful servant who has been part of the de Boys household for as long as anyone can remember. He warns Orlando that Oliver, suspecting that he will come home to his humble cottage, means that very night to burn it down with Orlando inside it. 'If he fail of that, he will have other means to cut you off.'

In other words he intends, by one means or another, to murder Orlando, so Orlando had better escape while there is yet time.

Touchstone   Celia   Rosalind

Adam has a hundred golden crowns hidden away. These he will gladly give to Orlando and follow him as his servant. He is 80 years old but still lively and vigorous and could not imagine spending the rest of his life better than by serving his young master. So off they go together and their steps lead them Arden-wards, to join the banished duke and his band of faithful followers.

Meanwhile Rosalind and Celia, dressed as man and wife, loaded with their belongings and followed by Touchstone, have also arrived in the Forest, footsore but happy. Here they meet an old shepherd called Corin 'in solemn talk' with his young assistant Silvius.

This Silvius is head-over-ears in love with a pretty little minx named Phebe, but she is proud and scornful and rejects all his advances, and Silvius can think of nothing to make her change her mind. Moreover, he refuses to believe that Corin did not endure just as many torments in his youth as he himself now suffers in the cause of love, and probably more. As the play continues we shall see just how badly Phebe does treat Silvius and learn just how grievously he does suffer.

Celia confesses to Corin how weary she and her two companions are, and asks if he can bring them 'where we may rest ourselves and feed.' Corin is not too helpful. He says he is shepherd to another man and does not shear the fleeces that he grazes, but since they are so weary they are welcome to come to his cottage and rest awhile. What nourishment there is at his little sheepcote they are welcome to share.

Then, as they walk along together through the Forest, he tells them that the sheepcote, the flock and the surrounding pastures are up for sale, which is just the kind of godsend Rosalind and Celia have been dreaming of. Without more ado they ask Corin to make an offer for this humble estate, and, if he succeeds in getting hold of it, invite him to come and work for them instead of his present ungrateful master; and we get the impression that Corin will be only too happy with this new arrangement.

We now plunge deeper into the trees when we suddenly hear the sound of music. One of the banished duke's courtiers, Amiens, is singing a song inviting everyone who thinks the way he does to join him in the Forest; to live under the greenwood tree and whistle in harmony with the singing of the birds. The only enemies they will meet are the biting winds and freezing cold of winter, and who cares about them?

Amiens

The Old Duke

The banished duke himself is also there, along with Jaques, a cynical and world-weary character who takes pleasure in undercutting everyone else's conversation with his special brand of world-weary philosophy. Thus when Amiens has finished his song he says, 'More, more, I prithee, more.' But when Amiens answers, 'My voice is ragged, I know I cannot please you!' Jaques replies ungraciously, 'I do not desire you to please me, I do desire you to sing.' He then pretends to be so bored by the whole proceedings that he gives a long yawn and goes off to seek some quiet corner for a nap. Scarcely has he gone than we find ourselves in another part of the Forest where old Adam, helped along by Orlando, is almost at his last gasp. 'Dear master, I can go no further. O, I die for food. Here lie I down and measure out my grave.'

Orlando bids him have courage. He will go in search of nourishment and if he fails to find any, only then will he give Adam permission to die, but not before! So Adam settles down to wait, wondering whether he was wise to have come on such a trek!

Meanwhile, Jaques has bumped into Touchstone whose conversation he finds vastly entertaining, chiefly because it is so very much like his own, except that Touchstone's observant and critical view of the world and its strange ways has none of the bitter edge that Jaques cannot help injecting into his. Together they go to join the duke and his courtiers for a bite of luncheon, just as Orlando bursts into their midst with his sword drawn. 'Forbear and eat no more!' he cries. 'I almost die for food, and let me have it.'

He then confesses that it is not for himself that he makes such an unmannerly demand but for a poor old man who, from loyalty and affection, has tramped with him many a weary mile. This old chap is even hungrier than Orlando and it is he who must first be satisfied.

'Go find him out. And we will nothing eat till you return,' the Duke replies courteously.

Away goes Orlando to fetch Adam, and, as the Duke remarks, 'There are in the world many people far more unfortunate than we are. Here in the Forest we've never had it so good!'

Shakespeare now takes the opportunity to write one of the most famous speeches in all his thirty-six plays – a speech in which Jaques shakes off his cynical and world-weary tone and the voice of Shakespeare himself, humorous and affectionate, lists the various stages that go to make up a complete human lifetime from childhood to the grave. First the baby, 'muling and puking in the nurse's arms', then the schoolboy 'with his satchel and shining morning face, creeping like snail unwillingly to school.' Next the lover 'sighing like a furnace,' the soldier 'full of strange oaths and bearded like the leopard,' the local justice-of-the-peace, well-fed and looking very serious and self-important, then the 'lean and slippered pantaloon' with his skinny legs, wearing well-worn

49

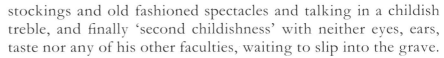

stockings and old fashioned spectacles and talking in a childish treble, and finally 'second childishness' with neither eyes, ears, taste nor any of his other faculties, waiting to slip into the grave.

This speech is twenty lines long, just enough for us to imagine Orlando going back to fetch Adam and returning with the old chap carried in his arms like a small child. The Duke welcomes them into their midst, sets food before them and bids Amiens give them another song. So now comes another of Shakespeare's beautiful lyrics,

'Blow, blow, thou winter wind,
Thou art not so unkind
As man's ingratitude.'

While Amiens is singing, Orlando confesses that he is the son of Sir Rowland de Boys and this gives the Duke great pleasure, for in former days he and Sir Rowland were good friends, and he bids Orlando and Adam welcome for the sake of this old-time friendship. Naturally the Duke asks Orlando how things are going at home. Has Frederick begun to mend his ways? And most important of all, how is his beloved daughter Rosalind?

Orlando tells him as much of the story as he dares; how he had thrown Charles the wrestler, how his brother Oliver threatened to burn him alive and how he escaped. As for Rosalind, he can only report that when he saw her last she looked wonderfully well and had been kind enough to praise him for his wrestling.

But at home Duke Frederick hasn't changed a bit! Summoning Orlando's brother Oliver to report on the tracking down of the runaways, he learns that there is no trace of them. Boiling angry, he tells Oliver that if he does not run them to earth very soon, all his land and possessions will be seized and he will be turned out of the kingdom. Oliver tries to make excuses but Duke Frederick is firm in his resolve.

Meanwhile the mention of Rosalind stirs in Orlando's breast a longing to see her again. Where is she now? And who with? Has she forgotten all about him and will he ever see her again?

For the moment there is no answer to these questions. The best thing Orlando can think of is to borrow pen and ink and some odd pieces of parchment from the banished duke, and start writing Rosalind little verses – as lovers have written to their girlfriends for thousands of years – then post them to her by nailing them on to trees, in the all-too-faint hope that she will somehow pass that way and find them. (He knows nothing of her banishment, so this is the best he can do and it eases his heart a little to do it.)

But who should come strolling through the Forest next morning but Rosalind herself, reading aloud one of Orlando's lyrics which she has plucked from a nearby tree.

As she reads, she walks into a clearing where Corin and Touchstone are discussing the relative virtues of life at court and in the country. Overhearing Rosalind reading Orlando's poems, Touchstone picks up the jog-trot pattern of the verses and adds a dozen or two lines of his own, making fun of Orlando's ardent style which begins,

'From the east to western Ind,
No jewel is like Rosalind.
Her worth being mounted on the wind,
Through all the world bears Rosalind.'

But Touchstone adds pure, awkwardly-rhymed, jog-trot nonsense – such as

'Wintered garments must be lined,
So must slender Rosalind . . .
Sweetest nut hath sourest rind,
Such a nut is Rosalind.'

Then comes Celia, also reading. She has caught a young man hanging verses on yet another tree, listing the virtues that many famous ladies in past ages have boasted, concluding that they can all be found in Rosalind, wrapped up in a single delicious bundle.

'Thus Rosalind of many parts
By heavenly synod was devised,'

– a synod being a special sort of tribunal, made up of monks or bishops or even, in the case of Rosalind, of angels.

Since they both have something secret and important to discuss, Celia tells Touchstone and Corin to move out of hearing.

'Do you know who hath done this?' asks Celia, coming straight to the point.

'Is it a man?' asks Rosalind innocently, and Celia replies, 'With a chain that once belonged to you, hanging round his neck!' At last, pealing with laughter, Celia breaks the news, 'It is young Orlando, that tripped up the wrestler's heels, and your heart, at the very same moment!'

Rosalind blushes. Then, oh how well Shakespeare understands the first thing she would say! 'Alas the day, what shall I do with my doublet and hose? Does he know that I am in this forest and dressed as a man? What is he doing here?' All the time her heart pounding with excitement.

'He looked as if he was out hunting,' says Celia.

To which Rosalind replies in mock ecstasy, 'O ominous! He comes to kill my heart!'

Just then they hear twigs being trampled underfoot and two male voices in lively conversation. Celia slips her hand firmly over Rosalind's mouth to prevent her speaking then pulls her into the shadows at the side of the path. There they stand listening, scarcely breathing.

At last the two men come into view, passing within a few feet of them, and lo and behold, as if in answer to Rosalind's heartbeats, one of them is the very man they have been speaking of, the man who not only comes to kill her heart but who killed it stone dead when he threw the wrestler on the palace lawn and bowed his head to let her hang her golden chain around his neck – Orlando.

Rosalind gives a sharp cry but Celia hisses her gently to keep quiet and they listen to part of the conversation. Jaques is begging Orlando not to disfigure any more trees by carving the name of Rosalind on them. Then he asks whether Orlando loves this young woman and when Orlando admits that indeed he does – dearly – Jaques says that it is a name he doesn't care for. 'There was no thought of pleasing you when she was christened,' replies Orlando.

It is clear that Jaques is not going to get much conversational change out of this encounter, so he leaves Orlando to unsheath his knife and start carving the word Rosalind yet again, this time on a beech tree, in prime copperplate – full of curves and curlicues.

So Jaques wanders off, slightly irritated at having met a young man who can top all his own half-baked witticisms with even sharper ones.

When Jaques has gone, Rosalind plucks up her courage, steps out of hiding and takes up the conversational challenge. But in her case Orlando has met his match, and this surprises him, coming as it does, not from a courtier or schoolteacher, but from a young and apparently simple country lad.

Gathering confidence, Rosalind pretends that she was educated by a learned uncle who taught her all the tricks of the conversational trade, especially those concerned with love-making. This leads her to bring up the subject of Orlando's verses, singing the praise of a certain young lady named Rosalind – verses which she pretends to disapprove of. She goes on to tell him how one can always recognise a man in love. He will have a 'lean cheek, a neglected beard, sunken eyes, stockings ungartered, shoes untied, sleeves unbuttoned, and everything about him demonstrating a careless desolation.' But there are none of these signs about Orlando and if indeed he is as much in love as his verses make him out to be and would wish to be cured, she knows the very remedy . . .

Orlando must pretend that she is his mistress and must visit her every day and try to woo her. Then she will give him a demonstration of the unreliable nature of typical women, 'be changeable, proud, fantastical, apish, shallow, inconstant, full of smiles, full of tears, will now like him, now loathe him, now weep for him, then spit at him, so that she will drive the young suitor from a mad humour of love to a living humour of madness' which will serve to 'wash his liver as clean as a sound sheep's heart, so that there is not one spot of love in it.'

'Just come to my cottage every day for a treatment,' she says, 'and I will guarantee a cure.' So persuasive is she that at last Orlando yields and they leave us looking forward to his first appointment.

Meanwhile Touchstone has fallen in love with a little country girl named Audrey, tending her flock of goats. She is bare-foot and tousled, her hands rough and her petticoat grubby. But she has beautiful black eyes and a winning smile, so Touchstone has decided she is just the girl for him. He has contacted Sir Oliver Martext, a travelling clergyman, who has promised to meet them and marry them and is prepared to do the job there and then in the greenwood. But Jaques overhears their conversation and persuades them that they would be more securely married by a proper parson. In the end they follow his advice and accompany him to the nearest village church.

The vicar is astonished to see such an ill-assorted pair. Surely Touchstone is not a baby-snatcher? Let them wait a year or two. A brief cooling-off period will make all the difference.

In the cottage all has been made ready for Orlando's first appointment but he is already late and Rosalind is getting impatient. Celia makes matters worse by saying that in her opinion Orlando is not true in love.

'Not true in love?' exclaims Rosalind.

'Yes, when he is in, but I do not think he's in,' replies Celia. Then, teasingly, 'He has come to the forest to meet the Duke your father and join his band of followers, that's all he's interested in.'

Rosalind's impatience is for a moment eased by the arrival of old Corin who tells her that if they would like to see a confrontation 'between the pale complexion of true love and the red glow of scorn and proud disdain' let them stand aside and watch the scene that is being played out between the two young people now approaching, Silvius and Phebe.

Silvius is in despair over Phebe's treatment of him, accusing her of being more cruel than the common executioner, who at least begs pardon of his prisoner. But Phebe is furious at such a comparison and lashes Silvius with her tongue. At that moment Rosalind, her eyes blazing with indignation, steps out of hiding and sets about Phebe just as angrily as Phebe has dealt with Silvius.

'Who might be your mother?' she says. 'That you insult and torture this wretched lad?' Then, turning to Silvius,

> 'You are a thousand times a properer man
> Than she is a woman!'

Then scolding Phebe,

> 'Down on your knees,
> And thank heaven, fasting, for a good man's love.'

Then she notices that Phebe has softened her expression and is looking lovingly at *her* instead of at Silvius. 'I pray you,' continues

Rosalind. 'Do not fall in love with me, for I am falser than promises made when one is a little bit tipsy.'

Lastly she invites Silvius to come and pay her and Celia a visit, adding under her breath, 'Shepherd, ply her hard,' meaning, 'Don't give up. Be strong and determined. In the end she'll give in.' Then she departs without giving Phebe another glance.

After this demonstration of the proper way to treat a conceited and unkind woman, Silvius plucks up courage and Phebe softens a little. It isn't going to happen quickly, but Rosalind has made a start.

'Your company used to irritate me,' exclaims Phebe. 'But now I shall try to put up with it.' She then proceeds to praise Rosalind, but eking out her praise with reservations, ends 'Some women would have come very near to falling in love with that young man. But for my part I neither love him nor hate him. What I'll do is write him a very saucy letter and get you to deliver it. Will you do that for me, Silvius?'

'With all my heart,' Silvius replies.

At last Orlando arrives for his appointment, swearing that he loves Rosalind so much that he would gladly die for her. But Rosalind contradicts him. 'The poor world is almost six thousand years old and in all that time no man has died for love. Troilus had his brains knocked out with a Grecian club. Leander went out one night to wash himself in the Hellespont and was taken with the cramp and drowned.' And she could, if she wanted, give him lots more examples. 'Men have died from time to time and worms have eaten them, but not for love!'

She then asks Celia to be a make-believe parson and marry them both, and Celia obeys.

'Will you Orlando take to wife this Rosalind?' says Celia. 'If so, you must say "I take thee Rosalind for wife."' No sooner said than done!

'How long will this marriage last?' enquires Celia.

'For ever and a day,' swears Orlando.

Then Rosalind chips in, 'Say a day without the ever. No, No, Orlando. Men are gay and lively when they woo, but cold and formal when they are wed. Maids are bright and shining when they are maids, but the sky changes when they are married.'

These scenes in Rosalind's cottage are some of the most enchanting in all Shakespeare, light-hearted and witty yet, since both are really speaking from the depth of their hearts, deeply moving.

Sometimes, when one half of her moustache would come unstuck and begin to flap, Rosalind would slip out into the little scullery to fetch a mug of elderberry wine or sloe gin, and when she had regummed the moustache into place, bring Orlando a nice cool drink – and right to the end he never guesses who she really is.

At last, Orlando says that he must leave for he is dining with the

Phebe

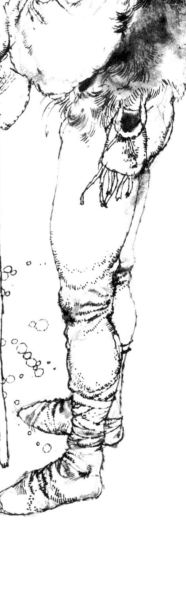

Silvius

Duke that evening; but he promises to return in two hours' time and Rosalind warns him that if he breaks one jot of his promise or comes one minute behind his time, she will think of him as the worst breaker of promises and the most faithless lover you could possibly find in the whole world, altogether unworthy of the young woman he calls his Rosalind.

When he has gone Rosalind confesses to Celia, 'Oh, coz, coz, my pretty little coz. If only you knew how many fathoms deep I am in love! I'll go find a shadow and sigh till he come.'

But she waits in vain for Orlando, and it is Silvius who now appears, bearing the letter which Phebe promised to write.

'My errand is to you, fair youth,' he says, handing the letter over.

Rosalind reads only a few lines then begins to laugh. This is not the 'taunting letter' Phebe promised to send her. It is clear that Rosalind's sharp lecture about her treatment of Silvius has caused Phebe to fall in love with her instead. As Phebe admits, 'when you scolded me I loved you. He that brings this love-letter to you little knows how much I love you.' She then begs Rosalind to accept her, body and soul. If she refuses, Phebe will be driven to commit suicide.

Rosalind fears that Phebe's treatment has turned Silvius into what she calls 'a tame snake'. In time he may manage to become a more determined suitor, but the omens are not too promising. In any event she's interrupted by the arrival of Oliver, the brother who had planned to murder Orlando by setting fire to his cottage after the wrestling match. He comes to tell Rosalind why Orlando has failed to keep his appointment, and a very strange story it is.

Walking through the Forest on his way to her cottage, Orlando
suddenly came upon a sort of tramp, a real drop-out, lying asleep
under an oak tree. A 'green and gilded snake' had wreathed itself
round his neck and was poised to strike its fangs into his mouth.
But suddenly, 'seeing Orlando it unlinked itself and slid away into
the Forest,' where a hungry lioness lay crouching, ready to leap on
the tramp and make a meal of him.

At first, he thought it was just a stranger lying there, but looking
closer recognised his own brother, Oliver. Twice Orlando turned
away intending to let the lioness do her worst. Oliver had planned
to kill him, why shouldn't he let the lioness kill Oliver? He was on
the point of doing so when his natural nobleness overcame his
feelings for revenge. He turned and, unarmed as he was, attacked
the lioness and overcame her, but only after a fearful struggle in
which his arm was badly mauled.

Oliver reports how there and then he embraced Orlando and begged forgiveness for all the wrongs he had done him, how together they went to the Duke's cave and bound up the fearful wound and how he, Oliver, explained to the Duke who he was and what he was doing in the Forest.

He then shows Rosalind a napkin stained with Orlando's blood, at the sight of which she faints. When she comes round they all agree she should be happy that the wound was no worse, for Orlando might well have been killed.

The play is mostly about love and lovers and Shakespeare who, like many poets, was very absent-minded, hadn't yet arranged a partner for Celia. Now he hits upon the perfect solution. Why shouldn't she fall head over ears in love with Oliver, and he with her? A bit sudden you may think, but that is why we use the expression 'love at first sight'!

Very shortly afterwards, we see Oliver is confessing to the bandaged Orlando his love for Celia and hers for him and their determination to marry. All that remains is to settle the time of the wedding, and most important of all, give Rosalind time to visit an old uncle she pretends to have discovered living in the Forest. She so much wants him to come and give his blessing to the great occasion.

Shakespeare now found himself in another fix. He had got two of his couples lined up – Touchstone with Audrey and Celia with Oliver. He must now find a way to make Phebe transfer her sudden infatuation for Rosalind to the unhappy Silvius whose love for her cannot be shaken.

To this end he gets Rosalind to promise Phebe that she will certainly marry her 'if she can,' but that if such a match proves impossible, Phebe will agree to give herself to 'this most faithful shepherd, Silvius'.

Phebe gladly accepts, for she cannot imagine what could possibly stand in the way of her marriage to Rosalind. Only Rosalind knows the answer to that puzzle, and the answer will be revealed as soon as she can change herself from a pleasing country lad into the beautiful young woman she really is!

First she sets a date for the ceremony. Why not this very night at full moon? Oliver will marry Celia, Touchstone Audrey, and Phebe Rosalind – if Phebe is still willing! The Duke has promised to give all three ladies away. But who can he give to Orlando? The lady Orlando adores is dressed as the handsome long-legged youth, who has been giving him love lessons in her cottage. But never fear, Rosalind promises to produce the right lady in time for the wedding, for this uncle of hers happens to be a great magician. He will arrange everything. There is nothing Orlando can do but trust Rosalind to keep her promise.

Without waiting for the others to agree, Rosalind and Celia disappear and go back to their cottage to change from their simple country dress into the glittering court costumes they brought with them; and half an hour later they come gliding through the trees in dazzling pink and powder blue, high-waisted and heavily flounced, both crowned with silver diadems that flash and twinkle in the moonlight.

For a moment Orlando stands in open-mouthed astonishment until, with a laugh like a peal of bells, Rosalind runs towards him, taking his hands and putting them round her waist in a loving embrace, and whispering once more the first words she ever spoke to him, 'Sir, you have wrestled well and overcome more than your enemies!' then falls into his arms. And suddenly the Duke and Amiens and all the band of courtiers – and even Jaques – are crowding round them, laughing and cheering and shouting their good wishes.

Only poor Phebe is greatly put out and gives a puzzled frown. She has been tricked! But she soon recovers when Rosalind detaches herself from Orlando's arms and comes across to kiss her, 'I did say "if I can"', says Rosalind. 'And if we found I couldn't, you promised to marry this dear faithful shepherd.' And she plants Phebe firmly in the arms of Silvius, indeed wrapping them around her as she has wrapped Orlando's round herself.

Now all is set for the wedding. Shakespeare has his quartet of lovers fully betrothed, only waiting for the Duke to tie the four knots. One of the courtiers dresses up as Hymen, the God of Marriage, and Amiens sings a beautiful song in his praise, saying how wonderful it is for a man to find both a cook and a bedfellow who can help him make some nice children to carry on the family name and comfort them in their old age. And no one is more thrilled than Rosalind who has at a single stroke, found a father and a husband.

There is only one surprise left in store for us. A messenger brings news that Duke Frederick has collected 'a mighty power' to invade the Forest, murder his brother and Orlando, capture Rosalind and Celia and Touchstone and put an end to this stupid open-air escapade once and for all. Indeed his troops have already reached the outskirts of the Forest when he falls in with 'an old religious man' who persuades him to abandon his evil ways for a life of prayer and contemplation. Frederick swears to restore his brother to the Dukedom and retire to a secret cave, where Jaques has promised to join him. There, together, they can end their days in prayer and noble thoughts.

The wedding goes forward, the Duke and Hymen between them cementing the four couples together amid a torrent of green leaves and wild flowers, accompanied by singing and dancing and ending with a feast at which all four couples profess their love and promise to be faithful to each other 'for ever and a day'. And the moon sets behind the trees before the merriment dies down and the lovers retire to sleep, locked in each other's arms.

58

So Shakespeare leaves us, the old Duke and his courtiers to return to the palace, but using the Forest of Arden for long weekends, Rosalind with Orlando, Oliver with Celia, Touchstone with Audrey and Silvius with Phebe, to have families and bring them up to know and love the Forest in which their parents had such exciting adventures before they were born.

The play was finished just in time for the manuscript to go to the scrivener whose job it was to copy out all the actors' parts, and Shakespeare took him through the whole play, pointing to places where his handwriting wasn't very clear.

When the company had their first read-through they were thrilled – such a lovely plot, such enchanting parts, such gorgeous situations – surely another big success for the Globe Theatre! So Master Shakespeare won his bet and the Mercer who had challenged him voted the play 'beyond praise' and delivered the ten yards of Damask to the Stage Door on the following morning. And the news soon got around that there was a new comedy on at the Globe and people had better go and see it while they had the chance. This they did and have been doing ever since, vowing that it is certainly as they like it. And I hope it is as you like it too!

Celia

Iago

Othello

Desdemona

60

Othello

Venice was one of the most wealthy and powerful cities of olden times, as well as one of the most beautiful; famous for her painters and architects, for her lovely churches and luxurious palaces, for her romantic waterways and sleek gondolas; but most of all for being a great trading nation, her merchant ships ranging over the whole of the eastern Mediterranean and far beyond. It was ruled by a duke and a group of citizens known as Senators, and one of these, Brabantio, had a lovely sixteen-year-old daughter named Desdemona.

In order to keep her high position in the world, the City kept a powerful fleet to carry her soldiers wherever they might be needed. And some of her finest troops were Africans, drawn from the warrior tribes of Nubia and Mauritania.

One of these Africans, named Othello, was so skilful and brave and loyal that he had been promoted to the rank of Captain-General, and wherever the battle was fiercest and the danger greatest, he was always to be found in the thick of it. With such a giant in charge of her defences, Venice felt secure.

Now in the course of his military duties, Othello often had occasion to visit Brabantio and, unbeknown to her father, Desdemona had fallen in love with him and had been seeing him in secret. Not only was Othello strong and handsome, but he had led such an adventurous life in his native land, and described it so vividly that she found him impossible to resist, and one night, swearing him to secrecy – for he would never have dared to do such a thing on his own – she had persuaded him to steal her away from home and marry her, then take her to his lodging, telling nobody but his standard-bearer Iago.

This Iago is one of the most evil characters in the whole of the world's drama, but gifted with a wonderful way of covering up his devilish nature with an open, honest and trustworthy face. For some time he has been expecting Othello to promote him to the rank of lieutenant, but Othello has chosen instead a young and handsome officer named Cassio leaving Iago to remain his standard-bearer. For this insult Iago hates Othello, and will do anything to get his revenge. And now his chance has come.

Desdemona's father will go out of his mind when he learns that his beloved daughter has run away with a Moor however handsome and brave and noble he may be. So Iago makes a devilish plan. He decides to wait till night-time, then take his friend Roderigo (a young Venetian gallant, stupid and dissolute) to awaken the old man and tell him to go and look into Desdemona's bedroom; and when he finds it empty, offer to take him to Othello's lodgings, because that is where he will find her.

Roderigo is only too happy to join in this piece of mischief, especially as he also wants Desdemona, and Iago tells him that if they can bring her father to tear her away from Othello, he may manage to get her for himself. And that is where the play begins.

It is moonlight. All is quiet except for the lapping of water against the timber landing stages and the signalling of gondoliers to their mates. Iago and Roderigo are hiding in the shadows outside Brabantio's house, Iago urging Roderigo to start shouting and hammering on the front door loud enough to bring the old man to his bedroom window, where he will learn that his precious daughter is missing. Roderigo can then offer to lead Brabantio to Othello's lodging where he will find her with her new husband.

Inside the house, there is sudden uproar as servants are roused and hurry to and fro along the corridors, lighting lanterns and candles and buckling on their swords.

Meanwhile Iago, to escape being seen, slips away to prepare Othello for Brabantio's fury. Hearing the clamour, Brabantio, clad only in his nightshirt and dressing gown, appears at the window and Roderigo challenges him to go and look in Desdemona's bedroom, then Brabantio will know whether he's telling the truth or not about his daughter's marriage to Othello.

But first things must come first. Lieutenant Cassio has already arrived at Othello's lodging to summon him to a meeting of the Senate. News has arrived from Cyprus, one of Venice's most precious protectorates, that a Turkish fleet is approaching the island. A naval force must be despatched at once to defend it.

Othello is about to obey this summons when Brabantio and Roderigo appear with a group of servants and attendants. Brabantio is in a towering rage, accusing Othello of being a foul thief, and claiming that he must have enchanted Desdemona or, he says, she would never have 'Run from her guardage to the sooty bosom of such a thing as thou, to fear, not to delight!' He then orders his attendants to draw their swords and lay hold of Othello and bring him before the Senate to answer these charges.

Othello, however, has no fear of Brabantio or the Senate. The services he has done the State will speak louder than all Brabantio's accusations. Besides, his affection for Desdemona is no trivial affair but true and heartfelt love, able to stand against all the imputations that can possibly be levelled against it. He will accompany Brabantio without bloodshed, knowing full-well that he can easily clear himself of all accusations.

But the threat to Cyprus is serious. The Duke and his Senators roused from sleep and dressed in a mixture of night-clothes and senatorial robes, hastily donned, are in full session waiting for Othello to appear, some sitting, some walking anxiously to and fro, when messengers arrive confirming that the Turkish fleet is certainly at sea and heading for Cyprus. This news is interrupted by the arrival of Othello, accompanied by Brabantio, Iago and Roderigo.

Brabantio, greatly distressed, is about to plunge into the story of Desdemona's seduction when the Duke breaks in with the news

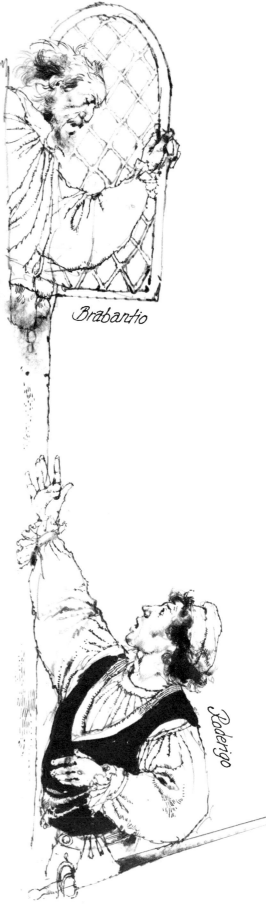

Brabantio

Roderigo

Othello

from Cyprus, telling Othello that he must, for the moment anyway, forget honeymooning and prepare at once to go to the island's protection. Only then does the Duke turn to Brabantio and ask why he is so perturbed. Brabantio hurriedly tells how his precious daughter has been stolen from him 'By spells and medicines bought of Mountibanks.' For, as he says, such a thing could not possibly have happened without the aid of witchcraft; and when the Duke asks who has been guilty of such an outrage, he points to Othello, who stands, magnificent and proud, against the crimson curtains.

Such is Brabantio's distress that the Duke and Senators now pause in discussing the danger threatening Cyprus, commanding Othello to explain in his own words the truth behind Brabantio's accusation. This he does, confessing how, whenever he came to their home to discuss affairs of state with her father; the building of new ships, the repairing of old ones, and the recruiting of fresh seamen to keep the navy up to strength, Desdemona had persuaded him to tell her the story of his adventurous life – the battles and sieges he had taken part in, the fearful dangers he had escaped from, how once he had been captured and sold as a slave and how he had escaped to venture even deeper into the heart of Africa. Desdemona had loved him for having been so brave in the face of danger and he had loved her for the sympathy she showed. That is the only witchcraft he has used. And here she comes to witness that his story is true.

Desdemona now enters with Iago, and in desperation Brabantio asks her where her true obedience lies. Without hesitation she confesses that she owes obedience to him for her gifts of life and education, but that was a matter of simple duty. Then she runs to Othello taking his hand, pressing it to her bosom, then her lips,

'But here's my husband!' she whispers, confirming that this is duty
and obedience of a very different kind. This is the man she truly
loves.

At this Brabantio sadly gives in, begging the Duke and his
fellow Senators to return to the threatened attack on Cyprus. It is at
once agreed that Othello shall gather a naval force and sail with all
speed to the protection of the island, and that Iago and his wife
Emilia (who is Desdemona's companion) shall follow him haste-
poste-haste, bringing Desdemona with them.

Here for the first time we learn how highly Othello prizes Iago
and how completely he relies on him. 'A man he is of honesty and
trust,' fully able to take care of his wife Emilia and of Desdemona.
Othello little knows what mischief is hatching behind that open
and friendly face.

Soon the conference breaks up, leaving Iago and Roderigo
together once more. And now Iago drops his mask of honesty and
begins, with dazzling invention, to spin the web that will enmesh
Othello in its ugly toils and help Roderigo to win Desdemona for
himself. He tells Roderigo that Desdemona and Othello are so
different, not only in age, but in temperament and character, he a
Moor, 'an erring barbarian' and she 'a super-subtle Venetian'; that
they will soon grow tired of one another, and that will be the
moment Roderigo must be prepared for. Let him disguise himself
with a false beard, bring a goodly supply of money and follow
Desdemona to Cyprus, along with Iago and Emilia.

Roderigo is quite taken with this bold and attractive plan and
promises to meet Iago early next morning prepared to set sail.

Left alone, Iago now takes the audience into his confidence,
outlining to us the first steps in his evil plan to bring Othello's
marriage to grief, and ruin his precious reputation. After a while he

will suggest to Othello that his lieutenant, Cassio, is becoming too friendly with Desdemona. He is both handsome and charming, just the sort of man women find attractive. Othello is of a frank and open nature but a very poor judge of people's characters. Yes, that's how he'll go about it! Let Hell and Night sow the seed and deliver the poison to the world!

On the quayside at Cyprus all is confusion. It is still blowing half a gale and Montano, the Governor of the island, along with a crowd of local citizens, is anxiously awaiting news of the battle. For the last hour they have heard distant gunfire. Maybe the Venetian fleet has been defeated and the Turks are already bearing down on the island.

All doubts are set at rest with the arrival of Cassio, whose ship, amid the turmoil of the storm, has become separated from the main fleet, but who brings news that the Turks have been vanquished and their ships wrecked or sunk. Scarcely has he delivered this

Montano

Cassio

news when a second boat arrives bringing Iago, Emilia and Desdemona, storm-tossed but happy. Desdemona is looking more lovely blown about by the wind than ever she did in Venice. Montano greets them but shares their anxiety that Othello has not yet arrived, while Iago tries to calm Desdemona's fears with some light-hearted banter about the relative qualities of men and women and the value of marriage, at the same time remarking to himself how tenderly Cassio caresses Desdemona's hand and what a perfect match they make and how this must surely lead to a caressing of a more dangerous kind.

Suddenly above the storm we hear a trumpet blast and Othello himself leaps ashore with the thrilling words, 'News friends, our wars are done! The Turks are drowned!' And clasping Desdemona to his breast and calling her his 'soul's joy', he gives voice to his deepest feelings as he holds her close: 'If it were now my fate to die this is the moment I would choose.'

Then, having been welcomed by Montano and his attendants, he bids them all enter the castle, to rejoice, to feast, and to rest after the fearful exertions of the battle. Only Iago and Roderigo remain behind to reveal the next stage in the plot to bring ruin to Othello's heaven-sent happiness.

When night falls and the castle guard are at their stations, Roderigo shall give Cassio enough wine to make him lose control of himself and start a quarrel, so loud that it will awaken the whole castle. And this is precisely what happens. Cassio drinks more than he can safely hold, loses his temper and starts a fight with Roderigo; and when Montano tries to separate them, Cassio turns on him instead, while Roderigo runs off to ring the castle bell and cry mutiny. In the fray Cassio gives Montano a nasty wound and he falls bleeding.

At the height of the clamour Othello enters and commands them to stop fighting. 'Hold for your lives!' he thunders, demanding to know how the quarrel started.

Iago steps forward and gives a brilliant account of the whole unhappy incident, true enough to be acceptable, yet false enough to put Cassio well and truly in the wrong.

Telling Iago he is sure he is trying to protect Cassio (though he is, in fact, doing exactly the opposite), Othello pronounces the deadly sentence, 'Cassio, I love thee but nevermore be officer of mine!'

So Iago has succeeded in the first part of his plot. Cassio has been demoted from his proud position as Othello's lieutenant and sits disconsolately cursing himself for having been so foolish as to accept that extra tankard of wine. Knowing how insanely jealous Othello is, it now remains for Iago to persuade Cassio that the only way he will ever get back into Othello's favour is by beseeching Desdemona to plead for him. Cassio gratefully accepts this advice. That is precisely what he had in mind.

Iago knows that if Othello sees Cassio and Desdemona alone together, Cassio could well appear to be pleading for her love and this will arouse in Othello 'the green-eyed monster, jealousy'. And Iago will do his best to increase that jealousy whenever he sees an opportunity.

The only thing necessary is that Emilia, who is to Desdemona more a friend than a companion, shall persuade her mistress that Cassio really deserves to be helped and that Othello shall catch the two of them talking together in the most intimate and friendly way. Then Iago's evil plan will be well on its way to success. And so it turns out. Othello sees Cassio and Desdemona talking together just as Iago has planned, then Desdemona comes begging Othello to forgive Cassio and take him back into his service. For a few moments Othello wavers. But Desdemona looks so pure and innocent that at last he yields to her request, 'Let him come when he will,' he says. 'I can deny thee nothing.'

This makes Desdemona very happy, for she knows how proud Cassio was of his privileged position and how much Othello valued his services.

As soon as Othello and Iago are alone together, Iago asks how long Desdemona has known Cassio. Othello answers that Cassio carried love letters between them both before their marriage and that therefore he knew her quite well. Then, using ambiguous words like 'seem' and 'if' and phrases like 'what dost thou think?' and 'why of thy thought?', Othello unwittingly helps Iago to build up one of the most fearful scenes ever written, dropping inch by inch into Othello's mind doubts about Desdemona's faithfulness, but always sprinkled with praise of Cassio's honesty, even ending with the lines, ''Tis fit that Cassio have his place, for sure he fills it up with great ability.'

Then, Iago leaves, apologising for having seemed to interfere in a matter so delicate as the relationship between Othello and Desdemona. Throughout this conversation, Othello has become more and more disturbed so that beads of sweat have begun to gather on his forehead and when, a few moments later, Desdemona enters with Emilia to call him in to supper, she notices this and takes out her handkerchief to smooth his troubled brow – a handkerchief of fine silk embroidered with strawberries – Othello's first gift to her and as such, doubly precious. Thus the evil seed is already sown. In his distress, Othello tears her hand away from his brow, the handkerchief falls to the ground and he rushes out. Desdemona, bewildered by his rough treatment, follows him and Emilia picks up the handkerchief.

This incident is the hinge upon which the rest of the play turns, for Iago has often begged Emilia to steal the handkerchief for him, but this, of course, she would never do. What she can do is to have it copied, give the copy to Iago and return the original to Desdemona. But at that moment Iago himself enters and snatches

Emilia

the handkerchief away from her, saying he has use for it – meaning that he can use it in the most horrible way. He will plant it in Cassio's lodging and let Cassio find it there. The poison he has dropped into Othello's mind is already having its effect. It only requires a few more drops in his bloodstream to set it boiling 'like the mines of sulphur'.

Soon Othello comes to believe all the suspicions that Iago has planted in his mind and behaves more like a caged animal than a civilised man. Grasping Iago by the throat he threatens to strangle him if the story he has told is false. But Iago braves it out for he now has a fresh trick up his sleeve. He tells Othello how, a few nights ago, he and Cassio shared a bedroom and how, in his sleep, Cassio spoke of his love for Desdemona, ending with the words, 'O cursed fate that gave thee to the Moor!'

Othello

He then invents the most vicious lie of all. Only a few hours previously he says he saw Cassio wiping his beard with the precious handkerchief, which he himself has snatched from Emilia and planted in Cassio's room in order to advance his slowly-developing plan for Othello's destruction.

This drives Othello into an uncontrollable rage in which he swears to kill both Cassio and Desdemona, forcing Iago to take the same sacred vow, ending by restoring him to the trusted position Cassio had robbed him of, saying: 'Now art thou my lieutenant!'

To which Iago replies, 'I am your own forever!'

Thus, inch by inch, we are prepared for one of the most distressing scenes in the play. By describing Desdemona's association with Cassio in the most brutal and ugly way, and by even inviting Othello to see them in bed together if he so wishes, Iago drives Othello to a sort of brainstorm in which he falls to the ground senseless, foaming at the mouth.

Here we see Iago at his vilest and Othello at his most helpless, unable to resist Iago's filthy suggestions which, moreover, he offers to substantiate by persuading Othello to hide in an angle of the castle wall and listen to a conversation he will have with Cassio that very evening.

The conversation concerns Cassio's girlfriend Bianca though her actual name is never used, so that with a few well-chosen words, like 'customer' which means harlot, Iago makes it sound as if Cassio has already been making love to Desdemona and that she even dreams of marrying him.

You can imagine the effect this has on Othello. He has already said that he intends to murder Desdemona but this scene in which he hears her described as a cheap little harlot planning to marry his lieutenant, settles the matter.

'My heart is turned to stone,' he says. 'I strike it and it hurts my hand.'

Despite the fact that he believes the whole of Iago's poisonous story and has already determined to murder his beloved wife and get Iago to murder Cassio, Othello is resolved to unravel every detail of his young wife's secret and unholy love. And this he can best do by questioning Desdemona herself, especially about the missing handkerchief, which was to him both magical and deeply personal, inseparable from his tribal roots. He bids her fetch it and she replies, 'Why so I can sir, but I will not now.' Then, fatally, she returns again to plead for Cassio. 'Pray you let Cassio be received again. You'll never meet a more sufficient man!'

This only drives Othello deeper into his certainty that she has betrayed him with Cassio. Demanding the handkerchief with ever greater ferocity, he leaves Desdemona standing dazed and uncomprehending.

Meanwhile Cassio has given the handkerchief to his girlfriend Bianca, asking her to make him a copy of it. This she refuses to do, angrily accusing him of having received it from 'some girlfriend'. This he quite truthfully denies since it was given to him by Iago; but Cassio pacifies her with the promise that he will join her for supper later that evening.

Determined to pursue his murderous purpose to the very end, Othello now bids Iago get him some poison with which to fulfil his horrible purpose, but Iago says, 'Do it not with poison. Strangle her in her bed, even the bed she hath contaminated,' meaning give yourself the pleasure of feeling her lovely body quivering with its last breath. 'As for Cassio,' Iago continues, 'let me be his undertaker. You shall hear more tonight.'

Their discussion is interrupted by a trumpet call announcing the arrival of two Venetian noblemen, Ludovico and Gratiano, with a despatch from Venice ordering Othello home and deputing Cassio to take his place in Cyprus. When Desdemona hears this she thinks it must mean that Cassio has been forgiven for his part in the quarrel on the night of their arrival and is now to be restored to his old position.

'By my troth I am glad of it . . . for the love I bear to Cassio.'

But this mention of love for Cassio only supports Othello's suspicion of her unfaithfulness and he strikes her across the face with the rolled up despatch, at which she bursts into tears and rushes away.

Unable to escape the torment into which Iago has driven him, Othello now seeks out Emilia, to get from her any fresh details of Desdemona's conduct that might possibly confirm her unfaithfulness. But Emilia is rock-like in her loyalty, proclaiming that if Desdemona could possibly be accused of unfaithfulness, any man's wife, however pure, could be. The husbands of the purest women in the world would be justified in believing such a monstrous lie.

But Othello is hungry for confirmation of his suspicion, not denial, and when Desdemona enters he drives Emilia out of the room and continues his savage onslaught, torn between self-pity and insensate fury, forcing her to her knees with the words, 'Swear thou are honest.'

'Heaven does truly know it,' cries Desdemona, to which Othello replies, 'Heaven truly knows that thou art false as hell.'

Without another word he storms out, leaving her weeping beyond control. She loves him past belief and cannot understand how he can have come to this state of mind. She thinks that the only person who might possibly help her is Iago. He is close to Othello, trusted by him, and wise in the ways of the world and when Emilia calls him in, he pretends to be sympathetic and understanding, ending with a gentle re-assurance that affairs of State make Othello bad-tempered and 'he takes his irritation out on you. Don't be troubled. It will soon pass.' So she goes in to supper comforted.

The one person not at all comforted is Roderigo, who accuses

Desdemona

Iago of having tricked him into believing he has the least hope of winning Desdemona and who threatens to expose the whole plot and beg her to forgive him for ever having entertained so unholy an ambition.

Now Iago has to think fast. Pretending to be greatly concerned, he begins by agreeing with Roderigo. Things have certainly not turned out the way he had intended. But if only Roderigo will be patient, everything will work out as promised. News has arrived that Othello is being transferred to Mauritania, leaving Cassio in charge of Cyprus.

If he and Roderigo can manage to dispose of Cassio, Othello will be forced to stay behind. Roderigo asks what Iago means by 'disposing of him' and Iago supplies the brutal answer, 'Why, by knocking out his brains.' Doesn't Roderigo realise that if they can get rid of Cassio, Othello will have to remain behind to guard the island and Desdemona will naturally have to stay with him? So Roderigo will still have an opportunity to seduce her? It is a complicated and rather heavy-footed ploy, lacking Iago's usual brilliance, but Roderigo thinks it worth trying.

In Othello's bedroom Emilia is helping Desdemona to undress and prepare for bed. As she does so Desdemona sings a bitter little song claiming that wives can be just as unfaithful to their husbands as husbands often are to their wives, and Emilia agrees.

'It's time husbands learned that their wives have just as much right to change their affections as husbands have to change theirs,' she says. 'So let them use us kindly or they may find their wives giving them a taste of their own medicine.'

Meanwhile, out in the street, Iago and Roderigo are waiting for Cassio to return from his supper with Bianca. At last they hear him coming and Roderigo darts out of the shadows and slashes at him with his sword. But Cassio's leather coat protects him so he remains unhurt and able to strike back, wounding Roderigo. Thus it is left for Iago to stab Cassio in the legs and bring him down, badly wounded and bleeding freely, then slip away into the darkness so that he shall not be seen to have had any part in the affray.

Hearing the uproar in the street Ludovico and Gratiano rush out from their lodging to see what is happening. They find Roderigo and Cassio wounded and bleeding and crying for help. Then from the darkness Iago appears as if he had just been passing and the noise had taken him by surprise. He knows that some of the groans come from Roderigo for he saw him being stabbed by Cassio. If Roderigo remains alive he will be able to disclose every detail of Iago's vicious plot. To prevent such a mischance, Iago immediately draws his dagger and stabs him to the heart, just as Bianca comes out to see what is amiss. Iago, knowing that Cassio spent the evening with her, immediately accuses her of having

Roderigo

Cassio

Jago

caused the quarrel that has led to this bloodshed. Then, arranging
for the wounded Cassio to be bandaged and carried in a chair, they
go to report the night's disorder to Othello.

While all this is happening a terrible drama has begun to unfold in Othello's bedroom. The window-curtains have been hurriedly drawn but they do not quite meet and a shaft of moonlight falls between them. Desdemona is lying in a troubled sleep while Othello stands in the shadows arguing the rights and wrongs of the fearful deed he is about to commit, weighing her beauty and her courage in marrying him against her father's will, against her deceit at secretly giving her lovely body to Cassio. That act of betrayal in the end blots out all other considerations and the whites of his eyes catch the moonlight as he throws to heaven a prayer for forgiveness at what he is about to do. She has deserved to die. Iago has supplied the proof. Honest, honest Iago! How fortunate he is to have had such a noble and loyal officer!

At last Desdemona awakes and bids him come to bed. He replies by asking her if she has said her prayers for he has come to murder her. She pleads with him. Why? Why? Why? What wrong has she done? In answer to her desperate pleading he accuses her of having given the precious handkerchief to Cassio, and that Cassio 'hath used thee.'

'How?' she cries. 'Unlawfully? He will not say so.'

'No,' replies Othello, 'his mouth is stopped. Honest Iago hath ta'en order for that,' not knowing that Iago has failed.

'Alas,' says Desdemona, 'he is betrayed and I undone.' She begs Othello to spare her one more night but he is adamant. 'But while I say one prayer,' she pleads.

'It is too late,' he replies.

Desdemona pushes the coverlet away, rises on to her knees and clasps Othello by the shoulders, struggling to kiss him.

'No, no, no!' she begs. But he forces her arms apart, seizes the pillow upon which her dear head was lying only a few moments before, covers her tear-stained face with it and begins to force it down, harder and harder and harder until there is no more movement. The deed is done. Only his own harsh breathing, mingled with choking sobs, can be heard.

At that moment Emilia, breathless and beating on the door, brings news of the fighting in which Roderigo has been killed.

'And Cassio killed?' asks Othello.

'No,' replies Emilia, 'Cassio is still alive.'

So Iago has failed. The one person who can testify to Desdemona's innocence is still alive. And so is the other. From inside the drawn bed-curtains Emilia hears a faint familiar voice, 'Oh, falsely, falsely murdered.' It is Desdemona speaking with her last breath. 'A guiltless death I die – give my love to my kind husband – oh farewell!'

Emilia then turns on Othello. She is a simple, brave and blazingly honest woman, who knows that Desdemona was 'heavenly true' to her marriage vows. Who has ever dared to suggest otherwise?

Desdemona

Othello claims that Iago has. 'And he is as honest a man as you
could find, a man who hates evil and corruption and dishonesty.
Not only is he your husband, he is also my friend and he is as honest
as the day.'

Gradually the truth sinks into Emilia's mind as she brings
herself to face the truth, that everything has hinged upon Iago's
slanderous reports.

'If he tells a filthy lie like that,' she says, 'his soul deserves to go
to hell and rot there inch by inch.' She then cries, 'Help! Help!' and
'Murder! Murder!'

Iago hears her cries and comes hurrying into the bedroom with
Montano and Gratiano. Emilia immediately flies at him in a fury,
'You told a lie, an odious damned lie! My mistress here lies
murdered in her bed, and it's your lying tongue that is to blame!'

All this time Othello has been standing in the shadows, stunned, waiting for the enormity of his act to dawn on him. Gradually the awful truth is borne in him as he recounts all that has passed, ending with his conviction that in return for Cassio's love, Desdemona gave him the sacred handkerchief, 'that antique token my father gave my mother,' and which Iago snatched from Emilia when she found it on the floor of Desdemona's room.

In a flash Emilia realises that the sacred handkerchief is the one which Iago took from her and which he has used to bring Othello and Desdemona to this terrifying pass. In desperation she cries out, 'Oh thou dull Moor, that handkerchief thou speakst of, I found and gave my husband. Indeed he had often begged me to steal it for him as he had a very special use for it.'

The game is now up. With a cry of 'Filth, thou liest!' Iago stabs Emilia in the back and rushes out pursued by Montano and Gratiano. Meanwhile, Othello remains stunned and empty. He now has nowhere to go. He appears to have shrunk from his tall, broad-shouldered self to a man half his size. His great and generous soul that was filled to the brim with love for Desdemona and then filled just as full with hatred of her, is now drained. He knows that the only chance he has of ever meeting her again will be on Judgement Day, and even then one glance from that beloved and most faithful of faces will hurl his soul from heaven and 'fiends will snatch it.'

Emilia

Othello

He is now holding her still warm but lifeless body, his tears tumbling into her braided hair; and calls upon those very fiends to wreak their vengeance on him, begging them to whip him away from the sight of Desdemona's precious body, to blow his soul to pieces, to roast it in sulphur, to wash the evil from it by plunging it into liquid fire.

Ludovico, Cassio and Iago now burst in, Iago held by guards, Cassio in a chair with his wound bandaged. When Othello sees Iago, he draws his sword and rushes at him, wounding but not killing him. Then Ludovico says to Othello, 'This wretch hath part confessed his villainy. Did you and he consent to kill Cassio?'

Othello agrees that he did and Cassio answers, 'Dear General, I never gave you cause.'

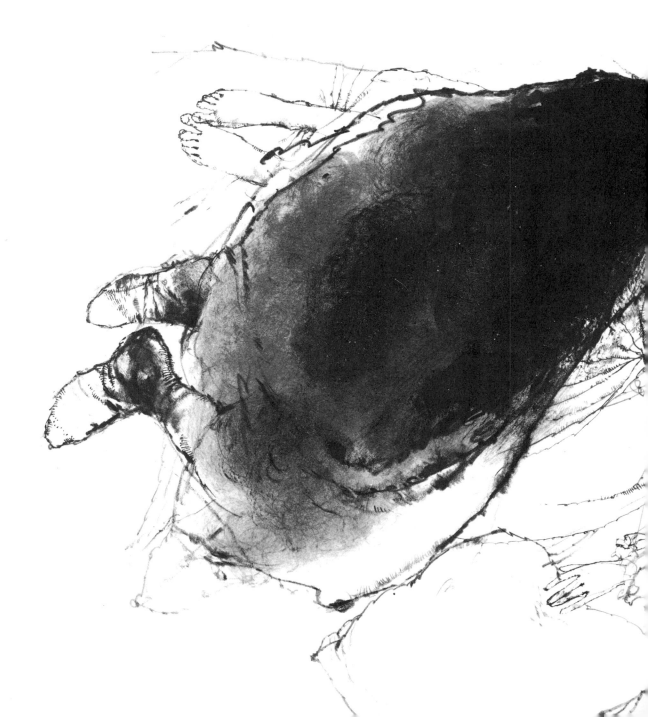

'I do believe it and I ask your pardon,' Othello replies, at which Cassio kneels and kisses Othello's hand, as if forgiving him for ever having doubted his loyalty.

At this a vast groan is torn from Othello and the tears begin to pour blindingly, uncontrollably, down his cheeks. He sinks down on his knees beside the bed, pulling Desdemona towards him, stroking her face and fondling her hair, still sobbing.

Ludovico, representing the Venetian Senate, now decrees that Cassio shall resume command of the forces protecting Cyprus. When he hears this, Othello staggers to his feet and begs to be allowed to speak a few words, not of excuse, but of simple explanation that Ludovico can report to the Senate.

'When people ask you how this tragedy happened,' he says, 'tell them that my love was too vast and too violent to control; that I am not by nature jealous, but when I have cause to be, it drives me insane. Tell them that I am like the base Indian in the legend, who threw away a pearl richer than all his tribe.'

Then, drawing a dagger, he plunges it into his heart, ending the tragedy with the words, spoken to Desdemona quietly and sorrowfully, 'I kissed thee before I killed thee and can think of no better way to die than to kiss thee again and die still kissing thee.'

And so he does, clasping the body of the girl he has so cruelly wronged.

Othello

Desdemona

79

Sir John Falstaff

The Merry Wives of Windsor

Pistol

One of the funniest characters ever to walk (or roll) on to the stage is Sir John Falstaff, planted by Shakespeare at the heart of his two finest plays, *King Henry IV, Parts I and II*. He weighs nineteen stone and a bit and leads a rowdy and rumbustious life in and around the taverns of London's Eastcheap. He eats like a horse and drinks sack out of all moderation. He cheats, he lies, he brags, he steals, he begs and he borrows (and rarely pays back) but he is so inventive, so ready to admit his mistakes, so full of wit and impudence that we love and cherish him in spite of all.

Sir John is surrounded by a small gang of old soldiers, Pistol, Bardolph and Nym; also by Mistress Quickly, formerly landlady of the Boar's Head Tavern in Eastcheap, where he even contrived to lure young Prince Harry, later King Henry V, into his company.

It is said that when Queen Elizabeth saw the two plays about her famous ancestor she laughed so much that she begged Master Shakespeare to write a sort of sequel showing 'the fat knight in love'; and *The Merry Wives of Windsor* is the result.

Hitherto, Shakespeare had written mostly of kings and queens and princes, of earls and dukes, what we would describe as 'high society', introducing the lower levels only to give contrast and a break from poetry into prose. Now he had a fresh idea. Why not a complete play about the middle classes, the grocers and shoemakers, the milliners and farmers, and the shop-keepers, 'the butchers and bakers and candlestick makers' as we used to call them when we were children. After all, they form the backbone of English life; why not set such a play in Windsor, in Shakespeare's day little more than a village surrounding the magnificent castle, but full of the simple, honest, respectable folk he had in mind? So that is what he did.

Pistol

It is winter. Falstaff has now retired after his long and riotous life in London, to Windsor, where he has settled in at the Garter, the best tavern in the village, leaving his three hangers-on, Pistol, Bardolph and Nym to shake down in the stables, bundled up in a couple of old horse blankets. His old friend Justice Shallow has sold his Gloucestershire farm and come to live in doddering retirement hard by, along with his young half-witted nephew Slender and a serving man named Simple. Round the corner another old friend from Falstaff's London days, Mistress Quickly, has got herself a job as cook-housekeeper to the local physician, a Frenchman named Dr Caius.

The other leading characters are Mistress Ford, her bosom friend Mistress Page, and their two husbands, George and Frank. Mistress Page is a local girl, born at Honey Pot Cottage in Wraysbury, only a few miles away. She met her husband Frank at the local madrigal club of which he is a staunch member, his rich baritone voice capable of a ringing Top G and even, if pushed, an A Flat. He has composed a sequence of 'Musical Ditties' for baritone and soprano, accompanied by lute, which is played by the local butcher Peter Sturgeon, and the three of them are much in demand at local festivities. Frank is good natured and open and generous and he and his wife are said to be the happiest couple in Windsor.

Master George Ford is an ex-seafaring man from Whitby in Yorkshire. He had served with Lord Howard against the Spanish Armada and met his wife in the kitchen of London's Guildhall when the City laid on a great dinner to celebrate the British victory. He is stolid and reliable and a fine stoolball player, but rather argumentative and madly jealous of his wife. Yet for all these differences in their personalities the families are firm friends, the two wives in particular feeling that God had intended them for sisters, which they would have been if the Recording Angel had not made a little mistake in the Celestial Register.

The play opens in the street outside the Pages' house. Shallow, his nephew Slender and Sir Hugh Evans, the village clergyman, all well wrapped up against the biting wind, have been invited to dinner with the Pages and are complaining that Sir John and his three hangers-on have been making a thoroughgoing nuisance of themselves, destroying the peace and harmony of Windsor by poaching Shallow's deer, beating up his gamekeeper and breaking into his hunting lodge. They have also made Slender drunk and picked his pocket while he was unconscious.

Sir John, who has also been invited to the dinner, admits all these misdemeanours but brushes them aside as worthless gossip, and all accusations and counter-accusations are forgotten and forgiven when Master Page and his buxom wife come to the front door to hurry the party in to dinner. Over a hot venison pasty they are to discuss a possible agreement for their beautiful daughter

Master Frank Page

Anne Page

Master Slender

Anne to marry Master Slender – who has been left very comfortably off by his grandfather, and is therefore, from Master Page's point of view, a very attractive prospect for a son-in-law.

The only problem is Slender who, instead of joining the party, stands dithering on the doorstep. When asked if he truly loves Anne and would like to marry her, he keeps saying that he is willing to be guided by his uncle Shallow. If uncle Shallow thinks it a good idea, he will fall in with uncle Shallow's wishes, especially if he can have his book of riddles as an aid to conversation with the dear girl, for he has no conversation of his own! Quite honestly he doesn't care one way or the other and even when Anne herself comes out to add her persuasion to that of his uncle and of Parson Evans, that he should come in and join the party, Master Slender is still unconvinced. It remains for Page himself to insist that dinner cannot be served until Master Slender joins them. So at last all are gathered in to partake of the feast.

Apart from giving Mistress Page a resounding kiss upon his

Sir John Falstaff

arrival and receiving in return a welcoming smile, Falstaff scarcely opens his mouth, except to eat an enormous dinner which he does with great gusto, I might even say with abandon. He is a vast human being, his belly so big that he has to wear a wide leather belt, fastened by a pair of buckles at the back and a pair of straps over his shoulders to hold it up. He is so fat, it is fully twenty years since he saw his own knees!

But what a dinner it is! What a pasty! A firm, savoury crust laid in an eighteen inch dish with six layers of sliced venison separated by layers of minced duckling, the whole flavoured with chopped onion, parsley and thyme. And then topped by a golden brown pastry overcoat, pinched into shape all round its edge, rising to a tantalising peak and glazed with beaten egg – with quart flagons of Castle Ale to wash it down. ·

But alas, discussion about the projected marriage goes very slowly. In order to bring matters to a head, Peter Simple, Slender's serving man, is instructed to take a letter to Mistress Quickly

Mistress Quickly

begging her to use her influence in speeding things up. Mistress Quickly is an old hand in such matters and a bit of rough-and-tumble marriage-broking is just in her line. She has had plenty of experience with Doll Tearsheet, the resident good-time girl at the famous Boar's Head Tavern in London. After a night in bed with Doll, half the bedclothes would be ripped apart as if a full-scale battle had raged and she had only yielded after a fearsome tussle. That is why Mistress Quickly has retired to the country for a little peace and quiet, leaving Doll to run the Boar's Head on her own.

After dinner, we meet Sir John at the Garter Inn, discussing with Mine Host how he can manage to cut down his weekly expenses. Mine Host offers an obvious piece of advice: 'Throw out one of your followers . . . Bardolph for a start. Let him make himself useful here – in the cellar and behind the bar.'

But that won't go very far to solve Falstaff's financial problems. Having learned that a friend of the Pages' named Ford is a man of means, he lets his cronies in on his plan to rescue his precarious finances. He will make love to Ford's wife and so get at her husband's purse! After all, a mere citizen's wife should be honoured to oblige a full-scale (nineteen stone!) knight, fresh from London where he boasts of having hob-nobbed with Royalty.

Sir John pretends he has already received inviting smiles from Mistress Ford and now he learns that her husband lets her manage all his financial affairs. Surely she will be happy to steal a few crowns out of the housekeeping money in order to pay for a little love from a bona fide knight!

What is more, our ageing gallant has his eye on Mistress Page, too. She also has given him an inviting smile, and she also looks after her husband's money. They shall be his 'East and West Indies', meaning that they will supply him with as much gold as the Elizabethan explorers are bringing home from the two sides of the world; and the idea of that makes him greedy. He will make love to both of them! He then reveals that he has already written letters to the two ladies (yes, to both of them!) in the most loving terms, and when Pistol and Nym refuse to stoop so low as to deliver them he instructs his little serving lad Robin to take them to the two ladies of his choice, the merry wives of our play. 'And deliver them in secret. Don't let their husbands see!'

It really is ridiculous. Mistress Ford and Mistress Page are no longer young girls but happily married women, in the full bloom of middle age, one thirty-nine years old and the other one forty-three, while Falstaff is approaching seventy-five. Besides, at nineteen stone he is grossly overweight! You would need a small crane to lift him. But like most fat men, he is proud of his stomach and forever patting it, evidently believing that it adds to his charm!

We now meet Mistress Quickly who, as I told you, has deserted the old Boar's Head Tavern in Eastcheap and taken a job as cook-housekeeper to the French physician, Dr Caius, living only a few yards away from the Garter Inn. Caius is a man of fiery temper, liable to fly into sudden unprovoked rages and is, at the moment, particularly sensitive as he is deeply in love with Anne Page and has just learned that he has a rival for her affections in the shape of Sir Hugh Evans, the local clergyman.

Mistress Quickly fully understands the letter Peter Simple brings to her for she claims to 'know Anne's mind as well as any woman in Windsor.' She is already committed to use her powers of persuasion on behalf of the Doctor, also of Sir Hugh, (who is forty-seven years old!) but (consulting her engagement book) thinks she may manage to fit in Master Slender. At least she will pencil him in.

But the Doctor overhears her conversation with Peter and, in a fury, decides to reduce the number of competitors by challenging Sir Hugh to a duel, to be fought not at some time in the future, but this very night, and fought to the death.

'By gad,' he yells, 'I will kill the jack priest. I will myself have Anne Page.'

Mistress Quickly assures him he need have no fear. 'Sir,' she says, 'the maid loves you and all shall be well.'

Nevertheless he rushes upstairs to change into his fencing gear, then charges off into the night to deliver his challenge. But rather than wear something warm, he goes out in a black all-over suit of kersey, a short woollen cloak and a pair of light shoes for swift movement. So he and his servant, who carries his foils, are already shivering before they start.

Servant

Doctor Caius

Scarcely is he out of the front door when Master Fenton arrives – he is in love with Anne, too, and has also enlisted Mistress Quickly's help in winning her, though not much help is really needed since he is the one that Anne really loves. The question is will he get her?

This Master Fenton is an undergraduate just entering his second year at Oxford. He's not a very good scholar, finding Latin and Greek particularly difficult, but is an excellent footballer and a good performer at the quarterstaff. So the Master of his college (Pembroke) has decided to keep him on for at least one more term.

Now we have Mistress Quickly working for Slender, for the Doctor and for Master Fenton, persuading them (as she regularly does), that they need have no doubt of Anne's affections, for she, Mistress Quickly, 'knows Anne's mind better than any woman in Windsor' and can guarantee that they shall all have a fair crack of the whip.

Meanwhile, Robin has delivered Sir John's love letters to Mistress Page and Mistress Ford – and what a letter it is! Just read it!

Dear Heart

Do not ask me why I love you. Love is not a matter of common sense. You are no longer young, neither am I. Surely that means we should have a strong feeling for each other. You have a lovely sense of fun, so have I. That should make our feeling even stronger.

You love a little tipple, so do I. That should make our feeling for each other stronger still. In short, if you feel you could love a soldier, I am your man!

Believe me ever sincerely,

Your own true knight
By day and night
Or any kind of light
With all my might
For you to fight.

John Falstaff

Master Ford in disguise

The tension between the parson and the doctor has now reached boiling point and both men have agreed to proceed with their duel. Mine Host, who has promised to act as referee, has measured their rapiers, but has craftily given them different meeting places some miles apart so that their anger may be directed at him instead of at each other; then, after a brief cooling-off period, they can shake hands and the duel need never take place, for, as an inn-keeper, he is a man of peace and would never risk losing good customers.

Scarcely has Mistress Page recovered from her mixture of astonishment and indignation at receiving Sir John's letter, than her friend Mistress Ford arrives, waving a similar letter and crying with laughter, for when they come to compare them, they find the two letters identical!

'Letter for letter,' says Mistress Page, 'only the name of Page and Ford differs. I'll warrant he has a thousand of these letters, written with a blank space for different names.'

Sir John has misjudged these two loyal and quick-witted friends. For a few moments the letters make them fall about with laughter, then they begin to plan how they will set about teaching Sir John a lesson for his impudence. 'Let's consult together against this greasy knight,' they say, and retire as they see their husbands coming.

Ford and Page are accompanied by Pistol and Nym who have taken offence at Sir John for asking them to act as postmen, and mean to punish him for this insult by informing the two husbands that Falstaff is planning to get both their wives into bed with him, either separately or together, for he is rascal enough to attempt either!

As Pistol says, 'He woos both high and low, both rich and poor, both young and old, one with another, he loves the gallimaufry,' meaning that he fancies all sorts.

Ford as you know is consumed with jealousy – and he believes it! He will, he decides, catch Sir John out by assuming a careful disguise. So the next time we see him he is wearing a little stick-on beard and a false moustache. Even his own wife fails to recognise him when she next sees him! He has also decided that when he meets Sir John it will be as 'Master Brooke' not as 'Master Ford'.

The two wives now confide in Mistress Quickly their plot to teach Sir John a lesson. She must report that Mistress Ford is madly in love with him and will welcome a visit between ten and eleven o'clock that very morning, when her jealous husband will be away from home. She must report that Mistress Page has also fallen in love with Sir John but that, unlike Ford, her husband is seldom away from home, so in her case it will not be so easy to arrange a meeting. However, Master Page has taken a great liking to Sir John's little lad, Robin. He will always be welcome at the Pages' and may come and go between them, using a password. If Sir John is patient everything will fall out as he wishes.

Mistress Quickly goes trotting down to the Garter and tells all this to Sir John, but even as she leaves, Ford (disguised as Master Brooke) is announced. With his moustache and stick-on beard and using a different voice, he is unrecognisable. Coming swiftly to the point, he tells Sir John that he has long loved the wife of a local citizen named Ford but that despite all the compliments he has paid her and the presents he has sent her, he has found it impossible to get at her. Yet he suspects she is far from being as virtuous as she pretends and if Sir John can only supply him with concrete evidence of her affairs with other men, it will drive her from her pretended innocence and give him a chance to approach her, and if he perseveres, to seduce her.

As an earnest of his honesty and good intentions, Ford hands over a bag of gold in advance and Sir John promises to carry out 'Master Brooke's' wishes to the letter; there is nothing he would *not* do for a bag of gold as heavy as that! Then he confides that he expects to be with Mistress Ford between ten and eleven that very morning and if Master Brooke will come to the Garter later that evening, he will tell him how much he has found out about her. This certainly brings a grim smile to Ford's face. Sir John has walked straight into his trap and he looks forward to catching this fat old rascal fondling his wife.

Frank Page is a different cup of tea. He is not worried. He will gladly turn his wife loose with Falstaff and he laughs at the very thought of her unbuckling the fat knight's belly-band and nestling in the arms of such a reprobate. But Ford says of his wife, 'I loathe to turn them together. A man may be too confident.'

In a field well outside Windsor, the doctor and his servant are waiting for Sir Hugh to turn up. Evans is already forty minutes late and the doctor is dancing about and thumping his own chest to help keep up the circulation. At last someone is heard approaching. It's not the parson but Page and Mine Host, along with Shallow and Slender who have all come to fetch the doctor home. For Mine Host, being a man of peace and the last person to encourage village enmities has, as you will remember, sent the two contestants to different locations – the doctor to this field, and Evans to Frogmore some miles away.

The doctor is furious at this deception, but Mine Host pacifies him with a promise that if he will come along to Frogmore and make his peace with the parson, he shall meet Anne Page and have a chance to persuade her that he will make the very best of husbands. Perhaps he might even be permitted to kiss her! At this prospect the doctor calms down and begins to feel grateful that he is still alive. So they go off together.

Meanwhile Mistress Ford and Mistress Page have been hatching their plot to deal with Sir John and are now putting it into action. Mistress Ford has sent her two servants, John and Robert, to fetch the huge laundry basket from the scullery; also a load of dirty

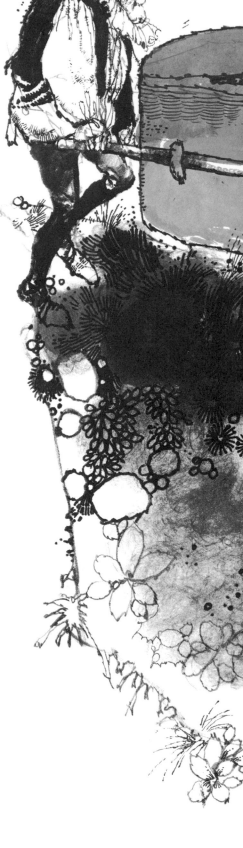

Robert

washing, shirts and petticoats and stockings and dishcloths and other odds and ends.

Suddenly little Robin, acting as advance guard to his huge master, enters and announces that Sir John, not wishing to be seen entering Ford's front door, is already approaching the garden gate at the back. On learning this, Mistress Page gives Mistress Ford a good luck kiss and flies helter-skelter out of the front door into an alley beside the house where she can peep through a small window and see everything that happens within.

The fat knight, panting with anticipation, bursts into the room and takes Mistress Ford in his arms, kissing her as if he would gobble her up, protesting that she is his honey-bunch and his heavenly jewel and that if only her husband were dead he would marry her and make her his lady.

Just as she is beginning to find it hard to hold him off – just think of trying to hold off a heavyweight like Falstaff! – Mistress Page, seeing that her neighbour is beginning to weaken, comes rushing into the house. She brings the dire news that Master Ford is approaching, accompanied by the Sheriff and a couple of constables, with 'half Windsor at their heels' to search for a gentleman whom Ford claims is now in his house, endeavouring to take advantage of his wife. Immediately there is panic. Falstaff, trembling with fear, must be concealed at all costs. But how? And where? That is the question. How to hide that mountain of a man?

It is Mistress Page who pretends to have the inspiration. Why not stuff him into the laundry basket, cover him with dirty linen and get John and Robert to carry him down to the stream at Datchet where the local women do their laundry? 'And tip him in?' whispers Mistress Page, 'That should cool his ardour!'

Out comes the basket and Falstaff eyes it doubtfully as John and Robert set it down. But when he hears the sound of the crowd approaching, he has no choice. In he is bundled and our two heroines squeeze him down till he fills almost every cubic inch of it. But they still have not quite finished. Now they grab the pile of dirty linen and stuff that in as well, filling the basket so full that they have to sit on the lid before John and Robert can fasten it down. But at last the job is done and Sir John is told to stop groaning, just as Ford and the Sheriff and half Windsor are heard banging at the front door.

John and Robert push the ash poles through the leather loops, lift up the basket and are on their way out of the house when Ford orders them to set their burden down; only when Mistress Ford, pretending to be amazed at her husband's wild behaviour, guarantees that the basket holds nothing but foul linen, does he let it pass through the door on its way to the river. But he now orders a general search of the house. And the whole crowd joins in the fun, hunting upstairs and downstairs, in every hole and corner. In vain. Sir John has escaped. But not to perfect freedom.

John

On the bumpy journey to Datchet he yells for John and Robert to unfasten the basket and let him out. But they guess he is only being punished for some wrong he has done their mistress, so they go tramping on with their load and only set it down when they arrive at the water's edge. There they unfasten the leather straps and turn the basket over on its side. With a roar out flies Sir John, headlong into the stream, making a mighty splash as he goes in.

When our two heroines (for so we must call two such loyal and resourceful ladies) have cleared the home of its uninvited guests, they collapse on to the settle, fighting not to split their sides with laughter and already planning another practical joke on their would-be lover.

'Shall we,' says Mistress Ford, 'send that foolish old Quickly to him, and beg forgiveness for having had him thrown into the water, then make up a new trick and catch him out a second time?'

'A good idea,' says Mistress Page. 'Let him be sent for tomorrow at eight o'clock, with our apologies for the disgraceful trick we had to play on him in order to prevent your dear husband from spitting him with his rapier.'

Then they peal with laughter once again, hugging each other with delight at their success in teaching Falstaff such a well-deserved lesson and wondering how he will survive his ducking.

In the street outside the Pages' house, young Fenton is busy putting his case to Anne, protesting how much he loves her and how faithful a husband he will be. But her father prefers Slender, largely because, as you will remember, he is comfortably off and Fenton has nothing to offer but his love. Seeing them there together, Master Page tells Fenton not to come near Anne again. On overhearing this, Mistress Quickly realises what a hot potato she is holding. For she has promised Slender, the doctor AND Fenton that she will speak to Anne in their favour! In the end she reassures herself in a typical workmanlike way: 'I will do what I can for all three of them,' she says, 'but speciously (she means 'especially') for Master Fenton' – and we get the idea that she rather fancies him herself!

In his rooms at the Garter, Sir John is complaining of his ducking. He is sitting with a towel round his head, his slops hanging over the back of his chair, his bare feet in a hot mustard bath and, between sneezes, complaining bitterly.

'Have I lived to be carried in a basket like a barrow of butcher's offal and thrown into the Thames?' he says. 'Well, if I be served such another trick I'll have my brains taken out and buttered and give them to a dog for a New Year's gift. The rogues toss'd me into the river as casually as they would have drown'd a blind bitch's puppies, fifteen in the litter.'

But he is cheered up by the arrival of Mistress Quickly who brings a heartfelt apology from Mistress Ford and a fresh invitation to visit her.

Robert

John

Sir John Falstaff

93

'Her husband goes out this morning bird-snaring. So it will be quite safe. She desires you to come to her between eight and nine and "have your wish".' She says, 'You shall have your wish' lowering her head in mock-shame and half-smirking. For this phrase sets Sir John on fire, as it is intended to do. He visualises the great four-poster and the scented sheets with plump pillows – all for his delight!

Never suspecting that he is dealing with two such clever women, Falstaff agrees. But no sooner has Mistress Quickly departed than in comes Ford (still disguised as Master Brooke) to learn what luck Falstaff had that morning. Sir John describes the whole unhappy incident of Ford's unexpected arrival 'with half Windsor at his heels', of being bundled into the laundry basket when he had barely begun his attempt to test Mistress Ford's virtue, of being carried to Datchet in a basket of foul linen and dumped into the river 'hissing hot'.

But this has not discouraged him, for he is visiting her again this very morning between eight and nine o'clock. Indeed he is already late for his appointment but he assures Master Brooke that this time he will succeed in overcoming Mistress Ford's modesty and that Master Brooke shall be a sharer in that victory. Let Master Brooke be patient and he will hear the outcome! But it is already approaching nine o'clock and Sir John must not keep his lady-love waiting.

Sir John little dreams that he is walking into a trap every bit as crafty as the trick to dip him in the river, for our two merry wives have already made a fresh plan to entertain him. Off he goes to keep his appointment, and before we have time to turn round he is cuddling Mistress Ford and telling her how beautiful she is and how faithful a lover he will be. Then Mistress Page comes hurrying in with a warning that Ford himself is already at the end of the street and will catch Sir John red-handed if they cannot hide him!

Sir John Falstaff

Mistress Ford

Once more in a basket? 'Never!' replies Falstaff. Up the chimney?
That is the first place Ford will look. In a coffer? A trunk? A chest?
A cupboard? A cellar? No, those are places he always examines. Sir
John is now trembling with fear and almost crying. If Ford catches
him he will beat the daylights out of him!

Master Ford

Then Mistress Ford pretends to have a brainwave. Her maid's aunt, a fortune teller known as the Fat Woman of Brainford, sometimes comes to stay with them, and has left one of her gowns hanging upstairs behind the bedroom door. If they can get Sir John into it, then find him a large muffler to hide his beard, and top him up with some kind of hat, they will surely get him safely out of the house. Sir John, eager to seize any opportunity to escape, staggers upstairs followed by Mistress Page to help squeeze him into the fat woman's gown, while Mistress Ford sits demurely on the settle pretending to be occupied with her needlework.

All goes as they have planned. Ford comes roaring in from the street along with Page, the doctor and Shallow. As they enter, Mistress Ford orders her two servants to bring the laundry basket and carry it out of the house as they did before. But Ford is not to be taken in again. He stops them and bids them set the basket down, then lifts the lid and starts tossing dirty clothes all over the

Sir John Falstaff

room, delving deeper and deeper to find Falstaff. All in vain. The fat knight is not there. But he may well be somewhere else in the house and Mistress Ford shouts upstairs, 'Come down with the old woman. My husband wants to come into the bedroom.'

'What old woman is that?' asks Ford.

'Why, my maid's aunt from Brainford,' replies his wife.

Down the stairs comes Falstaff dressed as the very woman Ford hates, a large muffler covering his beard and wearing a huge summer hat covered with hollyhocks, and a pair of old spectacles.

With a roar Ford grabs her and hustles her towards the street. 'Out of my door with you, you baggage, you pole-cat, you runnion,' he shouts, and picking up a strong crab-tree cudgel he begins to beat her bottom as hard as he can. Falstaff squeals with as feminine a voice as he can manage and runs for his life with Ford, Page, Shallow and the doctor at his heels and Mistress Ford and Mistress Page once again collapsing with laughter.

When all is quiet Mistress Quickly enters to congratulate them on the success of their morning's work and they ask each other whether it would be fair to play yet another trick on Sir John. Having decided to risk it, they sit down to dream up something suitable, and it is Mistress Quickly who comes up with a really good idea. Let me tell you about it.

There is a local legend that on certain winter nights, upon the stroke of twelve, mysterious things happen at an ancient oak tree in the middle of Windsor Forest. The ghost of an old-time huntsman named Herne appears, crowned with a pair of stag's horns and rattling a bundle of old chains, in celebration of the noble art of hunting – including, as in Sir John's case, hunting ladies! Thus the oak tree is known as Herne's Oak. And if the celebration goes well, fairies spring out from amongst the undergrowth and join Herne as he dances around the tree, rocking his horns to and fro and rattling his chains to show that he deserves to be as lucky in love as he is in hunting.

It is Mistress Quickly's idea that she will tell this story to Sir John and persuade him to dress up as Herne and go to the oak tree in secret just before midnight. If he does so in all sincerity, he will get his reward – all that he has hungered for.

'Oh yes,' asks Mistress Ford, 'and what is that?'

'Why you, Madam, you,' answers Mistress Quickly.

'What! Lure me into the arms of that old rascal?' exclaims Mistress Ford.

'Have no fear, you will not be ravished, I give my word. Your two husbands will be hidden near at hand. Carry this device through and you will be rid of Sir John's attentions once and for all.'

'Trust her, sister,' says Mistress Page, and it is agreed to let Quickly have her way. But first they must put their husbands in the picture, so they tell Ford and Page the whole plot, and they laughingly agree to play their part.

Mistress Quickly then ropes in Sir Hugh Evans the parson, bidding him collect a score or so of local children and dress them up to act as fairies, complete with lanterns, tapers and candles.

'Now,' says Mistress Quickly. 'I must persuade Sir John to undertake this one last trial. After the beating he got as the fat woman of Brainford, his ardour may have cooled. I will go see him.'

But Sir John is in no mood for apologies. 'Beaten black and blue,' he says. 'One dose of that is enough.'

'What about Ford's poor wife?' says Mistress Quickly. 'Has she not suffered? Has he not beaten her black and blue? As soon as you were gone. It will be a week before the poor wretch can sit down.'

At the thought of his loved one in pain Sir John begins to melt.

'But no beating can change her love,' continues Quickly. 'She burns for you like no woman I've ever known. Calls you her jewel and her heart's ease, and weeps and weeps out of all moderation.

But,' she adds, 'but – and there is much virtue in that simple word "but" – she plans to meet you in secret where she will reward you for the pain you have suffered in the only way a beautiful and generous woman can reward a man – especially a knight!'

She then tells Sir John the legend of Herne, promises to provide him with an iron chain and a pair of stag's horns, and to guide him in dead secret to the great oak shortly before midnight, there to await his jewel and get his reward.

Sir John's love for Mistress Ford is once more on the boil and he can scarcely wait till nightfall for the fulfilment of his dreams. He will gladly dress up as Herne and go through the ceremony.

Sir Joh

Mistress Quickly

'I will provide the chain and horns,' says Mistress Quickly, and she runs downstairs to let Mine Host into the plot. She borrows a length of chain from the cartshed and the great pair of stag's antlers which have decorated the hall of the Garter ever since King Edward III's reign. Mine Host will fix them on Sir John's head and Mistress Quickly will be on hand half-an-hour before midnight to lead the would-be lover into the forest. So far so good.

But Mistress Quickly is now in real trouble. She has promised to help all three suitors to win Anne Page; the doctor, Slender and Master Fenton, but can see no way of doing so. And it is Master Fenton, Anne's true love, who now takes a hand in the plot.

Knowing how Page favours Slender, and Mistress Page the doctor, and how he himself is so persistently repulsed by both parents, Fenton seeks the help of our friend the Host. He tells him how the two parents, unable to agree over the choice of a husband, have – separately and without telling each other – planned for their two chosen candidates, Slender and the doctor, to wait until the revels round the oak are at their noisiest and most confused, then seize Anne from the crowd and carry her away, one to the Deanery, the other to the little church over the hill. In other words abduct her and marry her.

'Now, without telling each other,' says Fenton, 'but each one telling Anne, her father plans that she shall be dressed in white, her mother that she shall wear green. And so as not to start a family quarrel, Anne pretends to agree with both of them, which means that she is really agreeing to marry one or other of two men she has not the least liking for – either Slender or the doctor – instead of to the one she truly loves.'

'And of the two she has no liking for, which one does she mean to choose?' says the host.

'Neither,' says Fenton. 'She means to choose me. Let me tell you how. We have found two village boys and let them into our plot. They will both be dressed as fairies, one in white and the other in green, and it is they whom Slender and the doctor will steal away to marry, one at the Deanery and one at the church. They have promised not to lift their veils until the wedding is well under way. Meanwhile, I shall have slipped a daisy chain around Anne's neck and fastened a crown of poppies in her hair. And so I will recognise her and it is she that I shall whisk away.'

'You have all things well arranged,' says Mine Host.

'All but a priest,' replies Fenton.

'Leave that to me,' says Mine Host. 'Twixt twelve and one I'll have the Vicar waiting for you here.' And thus it is arranged.

When it is dark, and the whole village supposed to be asleep, Sir John dresses as Herne and Mistress Quickly leads him into the forest. Meanwhile, Sir Hugh collects his band of fairies in the castle ditch with their lanterns and tapers and rattles all ready – including the two boys dressed in white and green!

Lastly, Mistress Ford steals out to join Sir John, caressing him lovingly and whispering into his ear sweet words of love and promising him a wonderful time as soon as they can manage to be alone together.

Finally, Mistress Page joins them in order to make sure of her share of his favours! But suddenly the clock strikes twelve, the fairies spring out of the castle ditch, humming like a swarm of bees, with their tapers glowing and their rattles making the Devil's own noise. At this Mistress Ford and Mistress Page give a shriek of mock terror, and break away to return to their waiting husbands.

The twinkling lights and the sound of rattles is so unearthly that Sir John believes the children really are fairies, especially when they swarm over him, pinching his neck and ears and his arms and thighs – singeing his grey hair and his hands and knees with their candles. Then, forming a ring, they begin their dance around the tree, and as they pass, Slender grabs the fairy dressed in white, not realising until they reach the oratory and the priest asks, 'Master Slender wilt thou have this woman to be thy wedded wife?' that it is 'a great lubberly boy' he has chosen. And the doctor grabs the fairy dressed in green. But, as you know, she also is a boy. Then Master Fenton joins the dance, next to the fairy wearing a daisy chain and a wreath of poppies in her hair, and at the next circuit he puts his arm round her and whirls her out of the dance and away they go together, to where the Vicar awaits them at the Garter Inn, and he ties the happy knot that makes them man and wife.

At last, when they are all gathered at the Garter, they all fall to hugging each other and laughing, all except Sir John who feels greatly put out, complaining at having been so shamefully treated, so foxed, so fooled, so foozled.

'Why Sir John,' says Mistress Ford. 'Do you think that even if we had decided to give up being faithful wives, that the Devil himself could ever have made you our fancy man? You, an out-sized suet pudding, puffed up with fat, a haunter of bawdy houses and taverns, an old soak like you?'

And dear old Falstaff confesses how mistaken he has been. 'I am afraid you have beaten me,' he says. 'You have brought me down to earth. You can do as you like with me now.'

He knows that he has done wrong and deserves to be punished. But Master Page unties the horns from his head and unlocks the chains from his legs, and bids him cheer up. Then invites him to join them for supper, to laugh at the jokes they have all played on each other. But Slender and Dr Caius arrive complaining of how they also have been tricked, and it takes quite a while to restore their good temper.

In the end Fenton and Anne arrive, close-locked in a loving embrace and they all go off to the Garter as if to a multiple wedding, with Mistress Ford and Mistress Page each holding one of Falstaff's arms to show that all his roguery is forgiven.

Sir John Falstaff

After these salutary experiences, Falstaff begins to change his wicked ways, gives up drinking (except for an occasional mug of sack), takes off fifty-seven pounds of excess weight, and gradually comes to realise that he is no longer his former vigorous self. So he moves out of the Garter and rents a little cottage on the outskirts of the village, and settles down with Mistress Quickly, there to end his days in peace.

At last, as he is nearly eighty, he dies. Mistress Quickly hears him talking to himself, so she runs upstairs to see to him. And there he is, fumbling with the sheets and smiling at his finger's ends and trying to pick the embroidered flowers out of the counterpane. So she knows the end must be very near.

Suddenly he shouts, 'God, God, God' three or four times. She tells him there is no need to think of God, not yet anyway. He asks her to lay another blanket over his feet because they are so cold. Then after a little while he goes cold all over and she realises that he has gone, 'babbling of green fields,' to King Arthur's bosom.

But what a life he has led! And how much fun he has given people! And how much he will be missed in and around Windsor, and what will they do at the Boar's Head in Eastcheap when they hear the news, and when shall we ever see his like again?

Julius Caesar

SPQR

Julius Caesar

For his Roman plays Shakespeare used the accounts given by a Greek historian named Plutarch, who lived and worked more than a hundred years after the events that the plays describe. So it is from Plutarch, translated into English at the end of the 16th century, that Shakespeare took the plot of *Julius Caesar*, an astonishing reconstruction of Caesar's murder by a small group of determined conspirators, and of the events that followed it.

The British have always felt an affinity with Rome. So much of our landscape and our language, our life and habit, stem from Roman models. So much of our sense of order and discipline and justice, so many of the words we commonly use are Roman (or Latin as we used to call it!) – for example *vinea* a vine, *portus* a harbour, *furnus* an oven, *taberna* an inn, *medicus* a doctor, *schola* a school, *populus* people, *arma* weapons, *castellum* a castle – and thousands of others.

The ground plans of many towns and cities in Britain – for example York and Lincoln, Colchester, Chester and Carlisle are stamped with the Roman pattern, along with roads, bridges, camps and settlements and country estates. Also much tesselated pavement has been uncovered, so many grave stones and statues brought to light, all bearing witness to the fact that we British still feel ourselves a part of the Roman Empire.

The political system of which we are so proud, our democracy, was invented by Greece but consolidated by Rome. Our code of laws is of Roman origin. When Rome was at her peak it was claimed that a child could walk alone from London to Alexandria unharmed, so firmly did Roman law prevail. This was achieved and held together by force of arms. The wild tribes from Germany and Scandinavia, from Turkey and Asia had to be driven back and held at bay while Rome, the mother city, was developing the framework to make all this possible.

Just before my wife and I built the Mermaid Theatre at Blackfriars in London, builders, preparing the foundations of a new office block nearby, came upon the remains of a Roman temple dedicated to the god Mithras who was worshipped by the Roman army. And thousands of city workers queued up to see it. A couple of young stockbrokers even knelt in the queue claiming that according to an edict of King Edward III, a citizen has the right to kneel and worship his particular god wherever he happens to find himself, and – producing specially designed identity cards – they claimed to be genuine Mithraists. So the policeman let them continue to pray.

In Lower Thames Street about a quarter of a mile west of London Bridge, about seventeen feet below ground level – the street level of Roman times – can be found the underfloor heating system or hypercaust of the Roman Baths. Britain was a cold country for Romans and they took the precaution of central-heating their homes. That meant plenty of running water, both hot and cold, wherever they settled.

In the late 1960s, when we were rehearsing in a room above the hypercaust, and the weather outside was boiling hot, my wife and I used to open the trap-door and go down to the bath level, eat our sandwiches, then take a forty-minute nap on lilos among the concrete supports of the original bathroom floor. On one occasion we actually stayed there all night, feeling ourselves highly privileged to be sleeping inside a piece of Rome.

I only mention this to remind you that wherever you tread in the British Isles or on the continent you will find fragments of the Roman world, the world in which the events of this play took place.

So realistically does Shakespeare capture the atmosphere of conspiracy in *Julius Caesar*, of men muffled up to their eye-brows, of conversations whispered in corners, of exchanged passwords, of the havoc that precedes and follows murder, that we could easily transpose the situation to the court of Queen Elizabeth I or James I (remember the men who organised the famous Gunpowder Plot?) or of Hitler or Mussolini. So deeply does he understand men of noble purpose, men envious, crafty, impetuous, loving, brave and loyal, that when this play is produced in modern dress – as it frequently is – we lose all sense that it was written about four hundred years ago and concerns events that happened twelve hundred years before that.

Inscribed on the standard of every Roman legion, and on the reverse of every Roman coin were the four letters, SPQR, standing for *Senatus Populusque Romanus*, meaning 'The Senate and People of Rome'. This meant that Rome and her mighty empire belonged not to a king or a prince or a dictator, but to the whole people. Rome was a republic, a *respublica*, something the people, if called upon, were happy to die for.

Caesar was a man of wide accomplishment, a scholar, statesman, and a brilliant soldier. He won many battles greatly extending the Roman empire and its influence, until people began to think of him as someone supernatural, even divine, which is the very opposite of democratic, more like dictatorship.

As a consequence of the praise and flattery heaped upon him, Caesar has begun to think of himself as being above common folk, and by so doing threatens to destroy the very democracy of which Rome was so burningly proud.

So a small group of idealists, led by Brutus, set out to prevent this from happening. And the only way they believe they can achieve this is by murdering him. So the hero of the play is Brutus who sees the danger to his beloved Rome and is prepared to give up his life in order to prevent it.

Julius Caesar is all about this precious word democracy and the tragedy it can bring if it is misunderstood or misused, even today.

Standard bearer of the Legion

The play opens with a bang. Caesar has had statues of himself set up all over Rome and a small gang of workmen are seen decorating them with coloured silks and ribbons, rather as people today put posters in their windows to show which political party they support.

It is a public holiday, and Caesar is riding through the streets of the city in triumph, to receive the thanks and congratulations of the people for his great services to the republic. A guard of honour awaits him on the Capitol – forty elephants drawn into two straight lines, each rider bearing aloft a torch, its flame leaping high into the sunlight. There are huge crowds everywhere. Men, women and tiny children adding their voices to the mighty roar that greets Caesar as he appears, cheering him to the skies.

This is a special occasion: never in the history of Rome have there been celebrations to rival this – chariot races in the Circus, athletic contests where the victors will be decorated by Caesar himself, a mock naval battle on a specially dug lake, wild beast hunts, fights between gladiators and, to cap it all, a battle between two armies, each five hundred strong. No wonder ordinary people love him.

Not everyone supports him, however. Two citizens, Flavius and Marullus, join the workmen and remind them that it is not so long ago that they were hanging decorations on the statues of Pompey, Caesar's great rival, whom Caesar has recently destroyed.

Suddenly the procession appears, led by twenty trumpeters playing full blast. Then a small group of cornus, the huge instruments wrapped round the musicians to the neck, the rich deep sound as if pulled up from the underworld. Then sixteen elephants, caparisoned in green and gold. Then half a legion of Caesar's special shock troops, the Praetorian Guard, their helmets and harness glittering in the morning sun. Next Caesar himself, along with Mark Antony, seated on thrones fastened to a low carriage, both turning and waving to the crowd – and whenever a greasy hand is thrust out, shaking it as if it were the hand of an old friend. Then come the Senators walking rather soberly, and among them Brutus and Cassius and Casca. Then another half legion of the Praetorian Guard, marching as if to protect Caesar from the rear.

Next two hundred prisoners of war, some roped together, others, ever ready to break loose and make a bid for freedom, chained, but ever and anon shouting curses on Rome and all her offspring. Then a group of Centurions and Praetors and Lictors, with civil servants and accountants, closely followed by the engineers, along with armourers and braziers, cooks, surgeons and priests. Finally an array of wild beasts, muzzled and led by slaves; tigers, monkeys, giraffes. Then a group of tumblers and jugglers. And last of all, a long stream of citizens – men, women and children all shouting 'Long Live Caesar!' And the noise! – the

The Praetorian Guard

Brutus

Cassius

roaring of the tigers, the trumpeting of the elephants, the screaming of the hyaenas and parrots mingled with the jangle of harness and the noise of the populace, is overwhelming.

And the man who has made it all possible is there, in the very thick of it – Caesar himself – a title that is to ring through centuries to come.

As they pass, a fortune-teller breaks through the crowd and cries out a warning to Caesar, 'Beware the Ides of March!' (The Ides being the fifteenth day of the month in the Roman calendar.) But Caesar says, 'He is a dreamer. Let us leave him. Pass!' So the procession moves on, leaving behind only Brutus and Cassius, who reveal that they, like so many others, are far from happy at the amount of power Caesar is claiming for himself and are wondering what they should do to curb it.

The two men are very different in character. Brutus, a true nobleman, thoughtful and sincere, with a passionate love of Rome.

Cassius, fiery and impetuous, pretending to love Rome as much as Brutus does, but at heart a born trouble-maker, envious of Caesar's success; but both deeply patriotic, both proud of the freedom their forefathers have handed down to them, and both resolved to see that it is preserved, whatever the cost, ready to fight for it. After all Caesar is only flesh and blood and no more worthy of obeisance than they are.

Cassius illustrates his point by telling Brutus how Caesar once challenged him to swim across the river Tiber when it was in full flood, dangerous for even the strongest swimmer. Although fully equipped as they both were, with forty or fifty pounds of armour, they plunged into the river, aiming to land on the opposite bank. But before they were halfway across, Caesar began to sink and would have drowned if Cassius had not gone to his aid and held his head clear of the water as he fought against the raging torrent. 'What kind of man is it,' Cassius asks Brutus, 'who can't swim better than that?'

On another occasion, when they were fighting in Spain, Caesar had an attack of fever and was so ill that he cried out for a cooling drink like a sick child. And yet, following his success on the battlefield, he is now treated, and expects to be treated, like a god, and ordinary men and women have to bow down before him and pay reverence to him despite his 'feeble temper'.

'I was born free as Caesar, so were you,' says Cassius. 'We have both fed as well and we can both endure the bitter cold of Germany and the blistering heat of Spain and Africa as well as he. When in all our history,' he continues, 'did one man deserve to lord it over Rome more than another? What a mockery it is that our beloved Rome should sink so low and we do nothing about it.'

Brutus is deeply moved by Cassius's passionate words and agrees that he will consider them carefully. He will say nothing more for the moment, but Cassius sees that he has shaken Brutus by his arguments, and he knows that they must give the matter deeper thought before they commit themselves to any rash or dangerous solution. Brutus is not quickly fired to action, but Cassius – angry and impetuous as he is – has struck a spark that, although only smouldering at the moment, will easily be fanned into flame.

Later, as the procession returns, Caesar notices Cassius and remarks how lean and hungry he looks, and how dangerous. If he were afraid of any man, he says, it would be a man like Cassius. But Mark Antony assures his friend that he has nothing to fear from so noble a Roman, and the procession continues on its way. As it passes, Brutus touches one man by his sleeve and asks him what happened on the Capitol. This is Casca, a man of biting wit and intelligence, who may well prove sympathetic to any action Brutus and Cassius may have in mind.

Casca tells them how Caesar was three times offered a crown, and that three times he refused it, each time more reluctantly than the last. And then, when he saw how the crowds threw their caps into the air and roared their approval, he had some sort of seizure, fell down and foamed at the mouth as if their cheering choked him.

'I have more news for you,' continues Casca. 'Flavius and Marullus have been put to death – for pulling decorations off Caesar's statues!'

From the dry and brutally frank way Casca talks, we see at once that Brutus and Cassius are not the only people to disapprove of Caesar's immense power. We also see that Casca is just the sort of man one would wish to have on one's side in a crisis. So it is not surprising that Cassius invites him to dinner later that night to discuss the matter further.

But that very same evening, quite by accident, Cassius and Casca meet again and events move swiftly forward. Casca tells him that on the morrow, the Senators intend to offer Caesar the crown yet again, only this time with the face-saving proviso that he may wear it anywhere throughout the empire except in Italy.

In a flash Cassius replies, 'I know where I will wear this dagger then. Better risk killing oneself than endure the slavery we shall bring upon ourselves if he is allowed to continue along the path he is treading.'

Cassius has now committed himself to open rebellion and, if need be, to Caesar's death. For a moment he fears that he has gone too far, but Casca agrees with everything he has said, and they clasp one another's hands in solidarity. If only Brutus could be persuaded to join them, their strength would be doubled. Was it not one of Brutus's ancestors who risked everything to rid the city of Tarquin when he was called a king? Surely the name of Brutus alone would add weight and authority to such an enterprise as they have in mind. All he needs is sufficient persuasion, for Brutus is loved and even revered by the people and his name would give their plot a firm moral foundation.

Cassius has already thought of this, and has prepared a leaflet stating their revolutionary aims, to be thrown in at Brutus's window, as if by some simple citizen.

All night Brutus stays awake, walking to and fro in his orchard, battling with the rights and wrongs of the fearful act he is contemplating. Finally he decides. 'It must be by Caesar's death.' But we are still not sure that he is convinced. Only when he reads the leaflet urging him to 'Speak, strike, redress,' does he finally make up his mind. For the word *redress* means to correct, to bring order to something disorderly.

'O Rome,' he says, as if taking the whole city into his confidence, 'if only this dangerous situation could be corrected, I promise you I will gladly pay my full share towards it, even if it means my death.'

Suddenly the conspirators arrive at Brutus's house, muffled up

The Conspirators

and with hats pulled about their ears – Cassius, Trebonius, Decius Brutus (no relation to our chief character Brutus but a clever and smooth-tongued diplomat), Casca, Cinna and Metellus Cimber. Cassius proposes that they should take a solemn oath to carry out their enterprise, but Brutus will have none of it. If their cause is true, and if they all believe in it, they need no oath to bind them together. Their simple word and the laying of hand upon hand is enough. To this they all agree, and thus confirm their determination to stand together come what may.

Only one thing troubles them. Would it not be wise to kill Mark Antony as well as Caesar? Antony is very close to Caesar; he is clever and brave and may, if they let him live, cause them a world of trouble. Cassius is all for killing him, but Brutus argues against it.

'Let us be sacrificers, but not butchers,' he says. 'Besides, Antony is wild, much given to sport and having a good time. He will soon forget the matter.'

So Cassius is overruled. Antony will be spared. But, as we shall learn, they will live to regret it. So the conspirators part, agreeing to meet on the morrow, when Caesar will be offered the crown once more by the Senate.

When Brutus is alone and the first light of dawn begins to silver the blue-black sky, his wife Portia comes to him, begging to learn, 'Who were these men who crept into our house so late? I can understand people trying to hide from the light, but these men were trying to hide their faces even from darkness. Who were they, dearest husband, and why are you so troubled?'

Brutus knows that Portia is completely trustworthy, so he embraces her and promises, when the time is ripe, to tell her everything.

In another part of the city, Caesar's wife, Calpurnia, is also deeply concerned for her husband's safety. He could face terrible danger if he goes to the Capitol as he has promised, for today is the Ides of March and Calpurnia has not forgotten the fortune-teller's warning.

It is difficult for us to understand that the Romans believed important events were signalled by strange happenings called omens. In other words, their lives were ruled by superstitions, and Caesar's wife Calpurnia is very sensitive to such signals. That night there has been a violent thunderstorm and strange sights have been seen: a lioness has given birth to a cub in the open street; a slave walked through the city with his naked arms aflame; blood has spattered down on the roof of the Capitol, and ghosts have been seen wandering round the seven hills of Rome – all omens signalling disaster. 'Let someone go and tell the Senators that Caesar is not well today, and cannot come,' she says.

At first Caesar is ready to take Calpurnia's advice, and when Decius, one of the conspirators, comes to fetch him, he tells him so. But Decius is taken aback, 'What will the Senate think when I tell them that great Caesar listens to such nonsense,' he says. 'Besides, it has been decided to offer you the crown once more, and to make sure that this time you accept it.'

This settles the matter. Caesar must not seem to depend on his wife's advice for everything he does. So when the other conspirators come to fetch him, he greets them warmly, and readily joins them on that fatal walk to the Capitol.

The conspirators have already formed their plan. When Caesar has made his opening speech, acknowledged the applause and made ready to receive the customary petitions, Metellus Cimber, whose brother Publius has been banished, will approach him with a request that Publius shall be pardoned and recalled to Rome. The rest of the conspirators will crowd around to support this request, which Caesar will almost certainly reject. They will all have daggers hidden in the folds of their togas, and will be close enough to make a concerted attack on him. And that is precisely what

Julius Caesar.

Calpurnia

happens. Metellus approaches Caesar and hands him his petition. Caesar gives him a long lecture ending with the words, 'I was determined to banish Publius and I am determined he shall stay banished.'

At this, Casca and the rest rush at Caesar (Casca from behind) and plunge their daggers into him. Only Brutus hesitates, pointing his naked blade towards Caesar, but not moving. Caesar, pouring with blood, and knowing that this is his end, has just enough strength to stagger towards Brutus with the words 'Et tu, Brute!', as much as to say, 'Not you as well, Brutus, whom I love and admire so much!' Then he takes Brutus by the wrist, pulls the dagger into his own body, and falls dead at Brutus's feet.

For a few moments there is a deathly stillness. The conspirators stand as if frozen, appalled at what they have done. Then, with a triumphant shout, they all kneel to wash their hands in Caesar's blood, laughing hysterically, and shouting for freedom and justice and the chance to vote on it.

Meanwhile Mark Antony, scenting possible danger for himself, flees from the Capitol, but sends his servant to ask Brutus why Caesar deserved to be murdered. He claims to have loved both Brutus and Caesar and has a right to know the truth. Brutus agrees to explain, and the servant goes to bring Antony into their midst.

The first thing Antony does when he arrives is to bare his breast to the conspirators, offering to let them do to him what they have done to Caesar: 'I beg you all, if you hate me for being Caesar's friend, now, while your hands are purple with his blood, do what you feel you must.'

This frank and courageous offer to let them kill him, as they have killed Caesar, quite disarms the conspirators, so that when he offers to shake each one of them by the hand, they accept. All he asks is that when, next day, they come to bury Caesar, Brutus shall not be the only one to make an oration. He, Antony, shall be allowed to speak as well.

Cassius, knowing full well how clever Antony is, and how unscrupulous, begs Brutus not to permit this. But Brutus overrules him, and the conspirators depart, leaving Antony alone with the blood-soaked body of Caesar. He now kneels, and begs the spirit of Caesar to forgive him for having been so 'meek and gentle with these butchers'. But, never fear, that was only

Cassius

Julius Caesar

pretence. He really intends to 'let slip the dogs of war' against them and take full revenge for the terrible deed they have done.

Before he can complete his curse, a messenger arrives with the news that Caesar's clever step-son Octavius – who will prove such a powerful obstacle in the path of Brutus and Cassius – is on his way to Rome. Indeed, he is only a few miles away.

Knowing that Octavius will prove a staunch supporter in the coming civil war, Antony tells the messenger to run back and warn him not to venture any closer until he has made his oration and can report whether it is safe for Octavius to show himself in the city. Everything will depend on how the citizens react to his speech.

Next day, the Forum is crowded and there is a stir of excitement as Brutus gets up into the pulpit and begins to speak, defending what he and Cassius and the rest have done. His oration is simple and logical and direct, with neither flourish nor decoration, giving an honest outline of the facts. He claims that he loved Caesar, but that he loved Rome and its precious freedom more, and that if the citizens of Rome now wish to do to him what he and his comrades have done to Caesar, he will accept their verdict and be prepared to die. It is for them to decide.

Antony

The crowd applauds Brutus's oration even as he speaks. It expresses exactly what they themselves are thinking – it is Brutus who should have been offered the crown, not Caesar. Brutus deserves a statue set up in his honour. They will bear him to his dwelling shoulder high. And so they do, shouting his name and calling on the gods to reward him and give him a long and happy life.

But as they run still shouting towards his home, they pass Caesar's funeral cortege, led by Antony, making its way to the Forum; and many of them begin to change their minds. They listened patiently to Brutus, surely Antony deserves to be treated just as fairly. So many of them turn back, following Antony, wondering what kind of oration he will make.

Antony, with two or three of his followers, now enters the Forum, carrying Caesar's body on a low bier, covered with a purple pall, and places it just below the pulpit. He begins carefully, taking pains to praise Brutus and the conspirators as 'honourable men', but slipping in just how much the people of Rome have benefited from Caesar's conquests, and how sympathetic he always was to them.

'When the poor were crying from hunger you would find Caesar crying as well. Would an ambitious man do that? But Brutus says he was ambitious, and surely a man as honourable as Brutus is to be trusted.'

He then reminds them how Caesar three times refused to accept the crown. Would an ambitious man behave like that? Then he breaks down, shaken with emotion; but at last continues, contrasting praise of Brutus and the conspirators as 'honourable men' with the fact that they allowed themselves to kill a man so noble and generous and so great a friend to the people of Rome. Thus he works on the emotions of his audience, gradually persuading them to see Caesar not as a tyrant but as a public benefactor and a true friend.

Finally, he comes down from the pulpit, pulls the pall from the body, and shows them Caesar's wounds, pretending to know which of the conspirators made the different cuts in Caesar's precious body, identifying each bloody gash with a particular name. 'Look, here's where Cassius stabbed. Here Casca drove his dagger in. Here Brutus struck. And his was the unkindest cut of all, for Caesar really loved and admired Brutus. When he stabbed, Caesar's heart burst and the blood rushed from the gashes in his body as you rush to your front door to find out who knocks so angrily and impatiently.'

He is, of course, lying, but you can imagine the effect his words have upon the already maddened crowd. And he has one more trick up his sleeve. He has managed to get hold of a copy of Caesar's will, and feels sure the citizens would wish to know how generous Caesar has been, bequeathing seventy-five drachmas to every single citizen, besides all his orchards, parks and private gardens, for them and their children to enjoy for ever. What a friend they had! What a friend they have lost!

At this, the listeners, who only a few minutes ago were cheering Brutus, are now ready to tear him and his fellow conspirators to pieces if only they could get at them. Indeed, one of Antony's servants hurries forward to report that Brutus and Cassius, getting wind of the disturbance and realising that the citizens are now turned against them, have ridden like madmen out of the city. Octavius, along with an old general named Lepidus, is even now at Caesar's house, ready to greet Antony and lay plans for the war that must surely follow. When they hear this, the crowds, who only a short time ago were full of praise for Brutus, even pressing forward to touch the hem of his toga, now scream with hatred, longing to find him and get their revenge.

The first man they meet in their headlong rush is a mild and innocent fellow named Cinna, by profession a poet. Now the conspirator who threw the leaflet into Brutus's window was also named Cinna, and the angry crowd is in no mood to distinguish between them. So, without further argument, they set on the poet and rip him apart. Thus Shakespeare shows his belief that a rabble of human beings is ugly and dangerous, not to be trusted to think clearly or make reliable judgements.

Brutus and Cassius have fled eastwards, each gathering a separate army ready to return and capture Rome. So Mark Antony and Octavius must collect an army and go in pursuit of them. But Brutus and Cassius have many friends and sympathisers who, now that the chief conspirators have fled, will use every means to take

Julius Caesar

119

control of Rome, either to restore them to their place of power upon their return, or to seize the city for themselves. These people must be dealt with, and soon Antony and Octavius are sitting down with lists of names and addresses, marking off those who must be got rid of. Many are their own friends and relatives, brothers and nephews and cousins. No matter, Octavius is a realist, this is no time for sentimentality. For safety's sake, they must die and although we do not see it in the play, we know from history that this is exacty what happened. It certainly shows that Octavius will stop at nothing to gain control of Rome.

We now learn that Brutus and Cassius have joined their armies and reached a place called Sardis, in what is now Asia Minor. Encamped there, they await the conflict with Antony and Octavius which they know must surely come. And here at Sardis they suddenly fall into a violent quarrel which nearly breaks their alliance. Let me tell you how this happened.

In order to raise money for their campaign, Cassius has become involved in dishonest dealings with local tradesmen, taking bribes for services rendered – something quite natural when moving a whole army from place to place. But this is something Brutus would never stoop to – and he has no hesitation in telling Cassius so, accusing him of corruption, then of being unbalanced and even cowardly – so much so that Cassius is at last driven to the point of baring his breast and offering to let Brutus, 'Strike as you did at Caesar, for I know that even as you struck you loved him far more dearly than ever you have loved me.'

Then Cassius claims that he is an 'abler' soldier than Brutus and accuses him of saying he is 'better' and they launch into a fierce argument over the difference between 'abler' and 'better'; it is like two schoolboys quarrelling.

At last Brutus apologises for having made Cassius so angry and explains that he is sick of many griefs, chiefest of which is that he has just received news from Rome that his beloved wife Portia, knowing how strong an army Antony and Octavius have gathered, and fearing for her dear husband's safety, has committed suicide by swallowing hot coals. This fearful news breaks through their quarrel and they embrace each other, promising that they will never again allow their differences to come to such a dangerous and unhappy pass.

A messenger now arrives with the news that the enemy is approaching, so Brutus and Cassius have to decide what tactics they will employ when the armies meet. Cassius is all for staying put and consolidating their present strong position – Brutus for advancing to meet them, hoping to gather reinforcements on the way. Once again, Cassius allows himself to be overruled, agreeing that in the morning they will strike camp and march to meet the enemy. So they bid each other goodnight and part.

Brutus is too troubled to sleep, so he decides to read a little until

Julius Caesar

Brutus

he becomes drowsy. But the taper flickers and a figure streaming with blood appears in the half light. Brutus strains his eyes and recognises the ghost of Caesar which has haunted him ever since that fateful day on the Capitol. Now it speaks – forewarning him that the coming battle will be fought at Philippi, away to the north-east, and that there they will meet again. Then it vanishes.

Brutus rouses his guards and security men. Did they see anything? A ghostly figure in the candlelight? No, they didn't even wake. Then to his boy Lucius, 'Did you?'

'No sir, I saw nothing. Perhaps you were dreaming.'

'It may well be,' says Brutus. But he cannot get the figure of Caesar out of his mind, pointing to his wounds and smiling as much as to say, 'You'll see. It will happen just as I said, at Philippi!'

Brutus is now wide awake and bids Lucius awaken Cassius and make ready to march. In their army were some of the finest soldiers in Europe, fully trained, protected by well-designed armour (helmets, breastplates, shields), equipped with razor sharp swords and spears, and accustomed to fight shoulder to shoulder in close ranks – not like the wild tribes from Asia who advanced in a mad rush, screaming for blood. Nor were the Romans afraid to die. They had taken over the ramshackle pantheon of Greek gods, giving them fresh names, Jupiter for *Zeus*, Venus for *Aphrodite*, Vulcan for *Hephaestus*, Bacchus for *Dionysus* and so on, paying only token respect to them, not true reverence. Along with Roman bravery went a simple brutality. Only when Christianity, responding to the gentler levels of the human personality took over, did the softer virtues of forgiveness and mercy begin to gleam in the darkness. But Christianity is still many years ahead, waiting to be revealed.

These were the armies and their leaders who faced one another at Philippi; brave, disciplined, loyal, skilful, but pitiless, asking no mercy when defeated, happy to inflict fearful punishment on the enemy when victorious.

The decision of Brutus and Cassius to advance instead of holding their ground proves disastrous. Here are no walls to batter down, but open country. It is cutting, slashing and stabbing amid the clash of bronze on bronze, the neighing of horses, the blare of trumpets and the low boom of the cornu – deeper than any brass instrument ever known – with rivers of blood gushing out to drench the thirsty soil.

The first to meet his Nemesis is Cassius. After a brief spell of fighting, Titinius, one of his trusted captains, is sent to report on what progress Brutus and his troops are making against Octavius. Titinius rides off and from the distance it appears that he is overwhelmed and Brutus slain. Hearing these fateful tidings,

Cassius commands his slave, Pindarus, to stab him. Pindarus obeys and Cassius falls dying, with the words, 'Caesar, thou art revenged, even with the sword that killed thee!'

But it is all a terrible mistake. Instead of having been killed, Titinius returns safe and sound to report that Brutus has been victorious. It was only from a distance – amid the dust and confusion of battle – that he appeared to be beaten. But, although victorious against Octavius, luck now turns against Brutus, who finds himself with a band of faithful followers surrounded and outnumbered by Antony's men, without hope of rescue.

It is a contest between youth and age, and it is the youngsters, Antony and Octavius, who are the masters. Cassius was a brave and experienced soldier, well into his forties, Brutus likewise of middle age, a man of high purpose and rigid virtue. But when it comes to the crunch, the young bloods sweep the old out of the way – Octavius to take the reins of power and impose his unique stamp of cold authority on the empire, Antony to fall victim to Cleopatra 'the serpent of old Nile'. Besides Antony and Octavius are out to get revenge. They have a debt to pay to one of the noblest men who ever 'lived in the tide of Times', and who was also their friend and kinsman. Thus their aim is furiously positive. Brutus and Cassius, being on the run are on the defensive and burdened with guilt, and that is no way to go into battle.

And, as if to confirm this, there in the dust of battle, Caesar's ghost appears again, pointing to the gash that Brutus made under his heart. And just as he had nodded when Brutus struck him, and again when he appeared in the tent, so he nods and smiles as if he at last is satisfied.

Brutus remembers his agony on the night he paced his orchard trying to weigh Caesar's life against Rome's precious freedom. He remembers Caesar's words 'Et tu, Brute' as he advanced and impaled himself on the dagger, and his thoughts turn to how he washed his bloodsoaked hands in the Juturna spring, not pausing until every single drop was washed away. He thinks of the suffering of his beloved Portia as she waited to die, and thanks the gods for having given him such a noble wife. Then he resolves to join her in that underworld spoken of by the Greeks, where ghosts meet old friends and remember what life was like on earth. He now has nowhere to go but into the dark. He had faced death many times before. He even had himself walled up in his own coffin for three days and nights as a test of his own courage and high purpose. Death itself could scarcely be a greater test.

Rather than bid his slave Strato kill him, he will kill himself. Strato has only to kneel and plant the hilt of the sword securely against a rock. Then whispering the words, 'Caesar now be still, I kill'd not thee with half so good a will,' Brutus falls, making sure that the blade runs up under his ribs and into his heart which bursts as Caesar's had done on that fatal day on the Capitol.

Octavius

When Octavius comes upon the blood-soaked body of Brutus, he cannot help grieving, for he knows what a fine man Brutus was and how much Caesar really loved him. Brutus would never have agreed to join the conspirators if he had not truly believed that Caesar's ambition for greater and greater power would be the ruin of Rome and its precious democracy. And Octavius tries to speak his feelings.

'Of all the Romans you could possibly name,' he says, 'Brutus was the noblest. Of all the conspirators he was the only one who did what he did, not from envy, but from love of Rome and the Roman people. It is a fine thing to be a man and to behave like one, and he of all men fully deserved the honour of that noble title.'

So they gather up the body of Brutus and take it to lie awhile in Octavius's tent, until he can arrange a funeral splendid enough to befit so noble a Roman.

Brutus